921
LOVELA- Wade, Mary Dodson
CE

        Ada Byron Love-
        lace

DUE DATE	**BRODART**	05/96	13.95

ADA BYRON LOVELACE
The Lady and the Computer

ADA BYRON LOVELACE
The Lady and the Computer

by

MARY DODSON WADE

A People in Focus Book

San Leandro USD
VI Funds

DILLON PRESS
New York

Maxwell Macmillan Canada
Toronto

Maxwell Macmillan International
New York   Oxford   Singapore   Sydney

This book is dedicated to Graydon the Elder, who since childhood has fascinated me with physics; Graydon the Younger, who knows the difference between Bernoulli and Fibonacci numbers; and Harold, alternate author of undecipherable equations, who played Lord Lovelace in the matter of the Bernoulli program.

Acknowledgments
The author wishes to thank Joanna Wood Schot, executive director of the Association for Women in Mathematics, University of Maryland, for her perceptive reading of the manuscript.

Photo Credits
Cover: Stock Montage
The Bettmann Archive: 10, 11, 33, 45, 48, 53, 74, 76. British Museum: 9, 40. John Murray Publishers, Ltd. England: 25, 109. National Portrait Gallery, London: 58. Nottinghamshire County Council, England: 103. Stock Montage: 65, 70.

Book design by Carol Matsuyama

Library of Congress Cataloging-in-Publication Data
Wade, Mary Dodson.
    Ada Byron Lovelace : the lady and the computer / by Mary Dodson Wade. — 1st ed.
        p. cm. — (People in focus book)
    Includes bibliographical references and index.
    ISBN 0-87518-598-3
        1. Lovelace, Ada King, Countess of, 1815-1852—Juvenile literature.
    2. Computer programmers—Great Britain—Biography—Juvenile literature.
    3. Women—Biography. [1. Lovelace, Ada King, Countess of, 1815-1852.
    2. Computer programmers. 3. Mathematicians.] I. Title. II. Series.
    QA76.2.L68W33 1994
    510'.92—dc20
    [B]   94-12678

A biography of the world's first computer programmer: Ada Byron Lovelace, daughter of the English Romantic poet Lord Byron.

Copyright © 1994 by Mary Dodson Wade

Dillon Press
Macmillan Publishing Company
866 Third Avenue
New York, NY 10022

Maxwell Macmillan Canada, Inc.
1200 Eglinton Avenue East
Suite 200
Don Mills, Ontario M3C 3N1

Macmillan Publishing Company is part of the Maxwell Communication Group of Companies.

First edition

Printed in the United States of America
10 9 8 7 6 5 4 3 2 1

/Contents

Note

In the Bodleian Library at Oxford University there is a massive collection of letters, diaries, and papers concerning the life of the world's first computer programmer, Ada Byron Lovelace. She was a programmer without a computer, for she lived 150 years ago and the program she wrote was for a machine that was never built.

The Lovelace Papers at Oxford were collected by Ada's son Ralph Milbanke, second earl of Lovelace. Ada's mother, Lady Byron, had assembled them in her quest to prove that she had been wronged by her husband. These papers, as well as the Somerville Papers at the Bodleian and those of inventor Charles Babbage in the British Library in London, reveal the life of a woman whose intuition allowed her to see beyond what was and to make connections to what could be.

Ada Byron Lovelace was the beautiful, eccentric daughter of one of England's most famous poets, George Gordon, Lord Byron. When he left England shortly after Ada was born, Lady Byron assumed sole control of their daughter's upbringing.

Nineteenth-century British society did not encourage women to use their minds. Ada, however, refused to fit into any mold. At the age of eight, she constructed model ships. At sixteen, she taught herself geometry. By the time she was thirty, she had written accurate descriptions of a new machine—the first digital computer. Even the machine's inventor Charles Babbage was astonished at the depth of her perception.

Ada's interest in mathematics, once a pleasant pastime, grew into an obsession. She became convinced she could make a great contribution to the world of science by presenting Babbage's Analytical Engine to the public. It did not happen. Babbage's machine was lost for a hundred years. Not until the advent of modern electronics did the computer finally become feasible.

Chapter / One

Child of Fame and Discord

The upper classes lived a privileged existence in early nineteenth-century England. Lords and ladies of the manor ran their huge estates like miniature kingdoms, overseeing tenants, entertaining guests, managing stables and farms. Each year they went to London for the spring "season," when the king and queen were at court and social life was at its gayest. Then it was back to the country estate—or perhaps to a fashionable seaside resort—for the summer.

It was into this exclusive world that Augusta Ada Byron was born. On Tuesday, December 12, 1815, the London *Morning Chronicle* announced that "Sunday last, Lady Byron was safely delivered of a daughter, at his lordship's house, Piccadilly Terrace." This daughter, born December 10, was the only legitimate child of the controversial poet George Gordon, Lord Byron.

Augusta Ada Byron

The handsome, twenty-seven-year-old poet was already famous when he married Annabella Milbanke on January 2, 1815. Just two years earlier he had received instant acclaim with the publication of the first two parts of a long poem called *Childe Harold's Pilgrimage*. Childe Harold was the perfect Romantic hero—handsome, dark, and dangerous, with a deadly secret in his past. His travels throughout Portugal, Spain, Albania, and Greece were based on Byron's own continental ramblings.

Not surprisingly, women often confused the poet with his creation. At the height of his fame,

George Gordon, Lord Byron

women threw themselves at Byron's feet. He was known for his riotous escapades and outrageous behavior. There were even rumors that he was the father of Medora, the daughter of his half sister Augusta Leigh.

Annabella Milbanke's personality was the exact opposite of her future husband's. Before meeting Byron, she had led a sheltered, straitlaced life. Inflexible, stubborn, and deeply religious, Annabella could also exhibit considerable charm.

Annabella, Lady Byron

She was interested in mathematics and had studied with a tutor, William Frend. During their courtship, Byron playfully referred to her as the "Princess of Parallelograms."

The letters Byron and Annabella exchanged during their engagement seem to reveal a mutual attraction. Yet each had other, less obvious motives for marriage. Annabella wanted to reform her rakish fiancé and make his behavior respectable. Byron, deeply in debt, may have contemplated marriage to the only daughter of wealthy, elderly parents in order to obtain her sizable dowry.

The Milbankes possessed a large estate. Annabella's mother, Judith Milbanke, had inherited the Wentworth estates and the Noel title when her brother Thomas Noel, Lord Wentworth died. The Milbankes immediately changed their name to Noel.

At first they seemed pleased to have such a famous son-in-law. Shortly after the marriage, Lady Noel purchased a dashing portrait of Byron dressed in traditional Albanian costume. She proudly placed the picture over the mantel in the drawing room at Kirkby Mallory Hall, the Noel estate in central England.

The bride's friends also initially rejoiced in her seeming good fortune. Annabella was marrying one of the most popular, romantic men in England. The groom's friends, however, could only shake their heads. They knew that Byron would not be tied down by marriage. Byron's best man, John Hobhouse, said that on the wedding day he felt as if he had buried his friend.

One sharp-tongued contemporary noted, "How wonderful of that sensible, cautious Prig of a girl to venture upon such a Heap of Poems, Crime, and Rivals." The groom himself remarked that his new wife was "a little encumbered with virtue."

It didn't take long for things to go sour.

Byron was temperamentally unsuited for marriage. Not long after the wedding, as the birth of his child approached, the poet's behavior became increasingly bizarre. A witness later recounted that in the hour before Ada was born, Byron began throwing furniture around in the room beneath which his wife was confined. When told that the child had been delivered, he rushed into the room and demanded of the new mother, "The child was born dead, wasn't it?"

Far from being dead, Ada was quite healthy. But Lady Byron had had enough of her husband's outbursts, cruel taunts, and drunken debauchery. She left his house when Ada was a month old and never returned. Byron left England shortly after the separation papers were signed and never saw his daughter again.

Lady Noel stripped the portrait of her son-in-law from its place of honor at Kirkby Mallory, shut it up in a case, and decreed in her will that Ada was not to see it until her twenty-first birthday, and then only if Lady Byron wished her to have it.

The sensational separation was the talk of Europe. In the nineteenth century it was unthinkable for a woman to leave her husband. Separation was cause enough for her to be ostracized from society, but Lady Byron took steps immediately to see that she and her daughter were not shunned. She started a lifelong campaign to make sure that the world knew she was the innocent party.

Chapter / Two

"Ada, Sole Daughter of My House and Heart"

After she left her husband, Lady Byron fled to her parents' home at Kirkby Mallory. But she did not remain with them long. She soon began a series of moves that lasted throughout her life. She could have lived in elegance, but she chose instead to live in rented houses, sometimes near London, sometimes in the countryside, sometimes near the coast. She went in search of good health, which always seemed to elude her.

Lady Byron was small and appeared frail. Although she was never seriously ill, she enjoyed consulting doctors. When she found one who gave her medicine she thought helpful, she visited or corresponded with him, keeping him up-to-date on her condition. Sometimes she would be bled. Doctors often used leeches to control a "fullness of blood," which was thought to cause all sorts of ailments.

Lady Byron had everyone convinced that she would not live long. As a child, Ada was often told that she must behave because her dear mother might die soon.

One doctor suggested that Lady Byron travel to improve her health. She seized this opportunity and set out, female companion in tow. Little Ada was packed off to her adoring grandparents.

The little girl was often sent to Kirkby Mallory. Sir Ralph and Lady Noel had been childless for fifteen years before Annabella was born, and they had doted on their daughter. Now little Ada became the center of their existence. During the happy times at her grandparents, Ada developed a lifelong love of animals, particularly horses and dogs.

Lady Byron left Ada with her mother so many times that Lady Noel was moved to chide her. Ada was not quite two when Lady Noel wrote, "Only a few days ago I took her into your Room, she looked round the bed and on the Bed, then into the Closet—seemed disappointed and said 'gone—gone!'"

Ada did not seem to suffer too much under the routine of her mother's extended absences, but she did grow to love her nannies. The first one, named Grimes, was especially attached to the little girl. When Ada was sixteen months old, Lady Byron wrote, "I give her dinner every day myself, though she will not suffer the nurse to leave the room without setting up a war-whoop worse than the Americans."

When Ada was two, she became ill with the chicken pox, and Grimes stayed up several nights trying to relieve Ada's itching and fever. Lady Byron was off on one of her trips and delayed her return, explaining to her mother, "It would be imprudent in me to return with any chance of taking the c. pox."

Ada's preference for Grimes infuriated Lady Byron. She assumed that the nurse had turned the little girl against her. She never considered that her own practice of cutting Ada's gums so that the child's teeth would come through sooner might have anything to do with it. For all of her kindness, Grimes was dismissed.

The young mother had very strong ideas about rearing children, and nanny after nanny was dismissed for failure to follow her rules exactly. Grandmother Noel was often left to see that her daughter's instructions were carried out while Lady Byron went off seeking cures for her many ailments.

When Ada was not with Sir Ralph and Lady Noel, they looked eagerly for letters giving details about their precocious grandchild. One of the first words Ada learned to say was *horse*. Lady Byron, staid as she was, lightheartedly reported to Lady Noel how Ada turned *horse* into a naughty word by leaving off the *h* and turning the *o* into an *a*.

Lady Noel sent an indulgent reply. "I am sadly shocked at dear Ada's mispronunciation," she said, and recommended "applying Birch to that part of which she speaks instead of Horse—Poor little Love! How Sir Ralph would laugh if he heard her!"

Lady Byron always feared that her husband would take Ada away from her because the British legal system recognized a father's rights over those of a mother. Her fears, however, did not have much foundation. Byron had said that he would not try to remove Ada from her mother. He only insisted that his daughter not leave England. The reason he gave was Ada's safety and comfort, but his real concern had more to do with his fear that if his child left England, his legal rights as a father would cease.

Lady Byron consulted a lawyer, and a way was devised to keep Lord Byron from ever gaining custody. Ada was made a ward in chancery. (Chancery was the law court that looked after children who had no other guardians.) This legal action provoked an angry letter from Byron, but he never returned to England to challenge the decree.

He was not, however, as thoughtless a father as might be supposed from his initial actions. Shortly after Ada was born, he intently questioned a nurse-

maid to find out whether the little girl had inherited his deformed foot and was greatly relieved to
find that she had not.

Now that he was no longer in England and had
no chance to see Ada, he was curious to know what
she looked like. He expressed that longing in the
form he knew best. Ada was a year old when the
third part of *Childe Harold's Pilgrimage* was published. Its opening lines ask:

Is your face like thy mother's, my fair child!
Ada! sole daughter of my house and heart?

Ada was Byron's sole daughter (at least the
only one he acknowledged) until the following year,
when Allegra was born in Italy to Claire
Claremont, one of Byron's lovers. Byron assumed
custody of Allegra because illegitimate children
were accepted in society even though their moth-
ers were not. Byron later placed Allegra in a con-
vent, where she died at the age of five.

On the advice of her lawyer, Lady Byron
refused to correspond with her husband. There was
no way Byron could ask her directly about Ada, so
he wrote to his half sister Augusta Leigh instead. In
a stiff arrangement that allowed him to find out
what he wanted to know, Byron posed his questions
for Annabella to Augusta. His sister, who was still

on speaking terms with Lady Byron at that time, relayed the questions to her. Lady Byron then responded to Augusta, who in turn sent the answers to Byron.

His mother-in-law also answered his letters at least once. Byron had expressed concern that something might be wrong with the baby's eyes. In those first few days he had observed that the child seemed to squint. Lady Noel replied indignantly that all babies did that.

Byron had no need to worry. Ada continued to grow healthy and happy. One day the chubby, rosy-faced toddler met the postman at the door. He exclaimed, "That young Lady has been painting her face I think." Lady Byron assured her parents, "Everybody is quite amazed at her magnitude and bloom."

The happy child busied herself with toys and pretended to do things she saw adults doing. Two days after her daughter's second birthday, Lady Byron reported to the Noels that as she was writing, Ada was tracing the letter *B* in her name.

Ada's temper sometimes flared when she was crossed, but not for long, as Lady Byron noted: "Her passions hardly ever last two minutes—their effect is to throw herself down, after a few tears she gets up and says— 'Wipe away her tears'— 'Kiss her'— 'I good.'"

Other quaint remarks were noted. When the little girl saw steam pouring out of a boiling kettle, she said, "Kettle's crying—Wipe away kettle's tears."

Ada was three when her mother became concerned about her daughter's imagination. She wrote to her old mathematics tutor, William Frend. "My daughter is a happy and intelligent child, just beginning to learn her letters—I have given her this occupation, not so much for the sake of early acquirement, as to fix her attention, which from the activity of her imagination is rather difficult."

Frend wrote back, "My eldest little girl gave alarming signs of being a prodigy, but I so effectually counteracted them that her mother began . . . to be alarmed when she was between six and seven years old lest she should be backward in her learning." In the nineteenth century, little girls were rarely encouraged to develop their intellectual capabilities, even when their parents were scholars themselves.

Lady Byron, however, was an exceptional parent. She later enlisted Frend's help in providing science and mathematical studies to help check Ada's flights of fancy. In the years to follow it was precisely the study of mathematics that became the vehicle for Ada's fantastic leaps of imagination.

Chapter / Three

No Weeds in Her Mind

Lady Byron had no worry about Ada's being backward. The child's quick mind seemed to absorb everything. By the age of five she could draw the shape of the earth. She could explain the words *parallel, perpendicular,* and *horizontal.* She could spell two-syllable words. She could even add sums of five or six rows of numbers. "There are no weeds in her mind," boasted her mother.

Lady Byron cultivated that mind. Wealthy children were tutored at home, and she hired the best tutors.

She also set forth progressive and common-sense instructions for Ada's governess. "The great thing is to be always calm and gentle, but steady and determined. . . . Be most careful always to speak the truth to her. . . . Take care not to tell her any nonsensical stories . . . above all never mention ghosts or such wicked folly. . . . If she happens to be hurt by any thing don't call it naughty, as if it meant to hurt her—which is very foolish—but soothe her tenderly & reasonably."

In contrast to that sensible advice, Lady Byron had other, stranger ideas about child rearing. She believed that children should be required to lie perfectly still for long periods of time. Ada was made to lie immobile on a board. If her fingers so much as moved, they were encased in black bags. It is not clear what the little girl was to learn from lying still. Lady Byron had a steel will, and perhaps she thought that her child could learn self-discipline by doing something she didn't want to do.

By age six, Ada had a morning routine divided into fifteen-minute sessions of arithmetic, grammar, spelling, reading, and music. In the afternoon she studied geography, drawing, French, music, and reading on a similar schedule. As time went on, geography became her favorite subject.

One day Ada made the mistake of writing in her journal that she did not like adding numbers. Her mother, who had a great fondness for mathematics, insisted on an immediate retraction. A subdued Ada wrote the required correction. "I want to please Mama very much, that she & I may be happy together. . . . One night I was rather foolish in saying that I did not like arithmetic & to learn figures, when I did—I was not thinking quite what I was about. The sums can be done better, if I tried, than they are."

Ada's reward for good lessons and behavior came in the form of "tickets" recorded in a ledger. Sufficient tickets earned a gift such as a book or picture. Sometimes Ada spent great effort on her lessons so that she could win back tickets she had lost through inattention.

She was not quite seven when her adoring grandmother died. Lady Byron then inherited the Noel name and estate. She and Lord Byron had not spoken to each other for years, but, as was customary, both added Noel to their names.

Ada knew nothing of her father. After she was grown, she confided to a friend that the one time she asked her mother about him, a terrible, cold anger came over Lady Byron's face. Ada never brought up his name again.

In spite of his absence, Byron remained curious about his daughter. Once he asked, through his sister, for a picture. After a year went by and he had not received it, he repeated the request. Finally Lady Byron had a miniature painted. From this, an engraving was made, which she sent to Ada's father. Byron then sent a swatch of his hair, which he wanted to be made into a locket for Ada. He specifically asked for some of Ada's hair so that he

The engraving of Ada, age five, that was sent to Lord Byron in Greece.

could see the color, because the engraving he had received was in black and white.

In passing, Byron suggested that Ada learn to speak Italian. He explained that, although he continued to write in English, he seldom spoke it. "Perhaps by the time that she and I meet (if ever we meet), it [Italian] will be nearly necessary to converse with me." The request was ignored.

When she was nearly eight, Ada began to experience severe headaches. Her vision became blurred. The agony of the blinding headaches kept her from her favorite activity of reading. When her father learned about the headaches, he was alarmed. The same thing had happened to him at that age, and he anxiously wrote Augusta Leigh to find out if Ada was all right.

He was also curious about Ada's "disposition, habits, studies, moral tendencies, and temper. . . . Is she social or solitary, taciturn or talkative, fond of reading or otherwise? . . . I hope that the gods have made her anything save poetical—it is enough to have one such fool in the family."

Lady Byron answered him by composing one of the "characters" which she wrote to describe people she knew. Not stooping to write to her husband directly, she sent a long letter to Augusta:

> Ada's prevailing character is Cheerfulness. . . . The impression she generally makes upon Strangers is that of a lively & perfectly natural child.—Of her intellectual powers, Observation is the most developed—The pertinency of her remark—and the accuracy of her descrip-

tion are sometimes beyond her years—
She is by no means devoid of imagination—but it is at present chiefly exer-
cised in connection with her mechanical
ingenuity—her self-invented occupation
being the manufacture of ships & boats—
& whatever else may attract her attention.

She noted that Ada was not particularly interested in poetry. This may have been a source of satisfaction to Lady Byron, who was trying to erase
from her child everything connected with her husband. Lady Byron then announced with pride,
"With respect to her temper . . . at an earlier age it
threatened to be impetuous, but is now sufficiently
under control." Ada had learned well. She knew
about being shut in closets and having black finger
bags placed on her hands as punishment for dis-
obeying.

Lady Byron included Ada's silhouette with the
letter and wrote, "Her person is tall & robust—her
features not regular—her countenance animated."
Just to let Lord Byron know that she was capable of
taking good care of her daughter, she went on to
say, "She is now in really good health under the
preventive system. . . . It consists of mild medicines
& a sparing regimen."

This letter reached Byron in Greece, where he had gone to help the Greeks in their fight against Turkish rule. In spite of his erratic behavior and unconventional life-style, the poet hated political oppression. At the beginning of England's industrial revolution, he had argued in the English Parliament against the death penalty for workers who had broken machinery. In Italy, he had given a large sum of money to arm the nationalists who were fighting against Austrian rule. Now he was a national hero in Greece for championing their cause.

Byron proudly showed Ada's silhouette to his Greek comrades. He wrote Augusta of his joy at learning that his daughter liked to construct mechanical toys. He too had enjoyed building things when he was a child.

Two months later, on April 19, 1824, George Gordon Noel, Lord Byron died of a fever. On his writing desk lay the letter containing the description of his daughter.

Byron's body was shipped back to England. On a strange impulse, Lady Byron wrote a poem lamenting the authorities' refusal to grant her husband the honor of being buried in the Poet's Corner at Westminster Abbey. She was not sufficiently moved, however, to go to the London funeral. Nor did she allow Ada to attend Byron's burial near

Newstead Abbey in Nottinghamshire.

Eight-year-old Ada still did not know anything about her father. To Lady Byron's credit, she never spoke ill of him in front of the child. She simply maintained a stony silence.

It would be years before Ada saw the forbidden portrait at Kirkby Mallory, and still longer before she visited Newstead Abbey and her father's burial place.

Chapter / Four

Proper Education

Soon after Byron's death, Lady Byron's father died. Her inheritance as a widow and as an only child gave her an annual income amounting to £7,000 in a time when an income of £1,000 per year was considered excellent. With money to spend and the freedom to spend it anywhere she chose, Lady Byron began a tour of the Continent with her eleven-year-old daughter.

For two years they traveled through Holland, Germany, Italy, Switzerland, and France, visiting museums and historic places. The two travelers were recognized everywhere they went and they made no effort to hide their identity. Curious onlookers stared at Ada to see if the young girl had inherited her father's handsome features. They found little resemblance as they looked at the gawky girl.

When mother and daughter returned to England in 1828, Ada continued her studies. Lady Byron went to great trouble to provide tutors for her daughter, although for a while she toyed with the idea of allowing Ada to participate in a novel form of education similar to that practiced at Hofwyl, a boys' school located near Berne, Switzerland.

Hofwyl was run on the principle of "education by action." The school accepted both "highborn" and "lowborn" students, and all of the boys, rich or poor, had to participate in activities.

The lower-class students got up at three in the morning and performed agricultural chores, worked in the leather shop, or did carpentry or something mechanical. Upper-class students participated in military exercises, swam, rode, skated, or gardened.

If one of the upper-class boys needed still more activity, he was sent to work in the fields with students from the lower school. Lady Byron thought this form of education was helpful to society. "The sons of the wealthy thus learnt to respect labour in the persons of the pupils of the poor school; whilst on the other hand the poor learnt to view their richer companions, not as enemies, but as sympathizing friends."

As part of her program for improving society,

Lady Byron established Ealing Grove, a boys'
school similar to Hofwyl, just west of London. Ada
did not actually attend this school with lower-class
students, but her mother considered having Ada
make her own shoes. The project died when it was
pointed out that doing so would be more expensive
than purchasing them.

Just as Ada entered her teen years, a new interest captured Lady Byron's attention. The "science"
of phrenology was sweeping across England.
Phrenologists claimed that the shape of one's head
revealed personality traits. Different skills and
attributes were assigned to particular parts of the
skull. If the skull was thick in one area, it meant
that the person had a great deal of a certain ability
or attribute because, experts explained, the skull
grew to its shape over the brain underneath.

Lady Byron consulted a phrenologist and was
very pleased that he had understood right away
that "sensitiveness" to the opinions of others was
one of her main attributes. Ada learned that the
bumps on her head revealed a personality ruled by
"imagination," "wonder," and "very high intellectual powers."

Lady Byron was convinced of the accuracy of
phrenology, and she chose her friends by the shape
of their heads. She particularly looked for people
with high foreheads; it meant they were given to

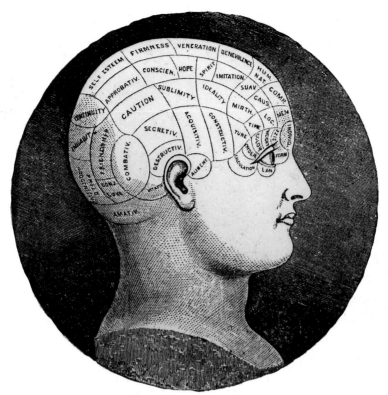

The "science" of phrenology was all the rage in the nineteenth century. Bumps on the head were supposed to reveal personality traits.

veneration and benevolence.

Lady Byron was given to benevolence herself. Besides her boys' school, she spent time touring penitentiaries and insane asylums. Her only wish, she said, was to lead a godly life.

Many of her friends considered her a saint, but her servants knew she could be a tyrant. Twice, the entire staff in her house resigned. This was unthinkable when employees depended on references from a previous employer in order to obtain a new position.

Ada, meanwhile, continued lessons with her tutors. Reading was still her favorite occupation.

She also studied several languages, including Latin. And she began to study under Lady Byron's old mathematics teacher, William Frend.

Frend had caused quite a stir many years before when he was a student at Cambridge University. He announced his faith in the Unitarian doctrine, which asserts that God has only one person rather than three, as preached by the Church of England. Cambridge dismissed Frend for publishing a pamphlet with such unorthodox religious views.

Thirteen-year-old Ada began to correspond with the elderly tutor, who guided her in astronomy and algebra. His letters often included religious admonitions, but they were mild considering the lectures Ada received from some of her mother's friends.

The young pupil soon was studying mathematics that went beyond Frend's comprehension. Frend refused to consider the concept of negative numbers. He maintained that thinking about imaginary or symbolic numbers could only foster superstition.

The old mathematician was on safer ground with astronomy. He sent Ada directions for making a planetarium and told her about upcoming eclipses and star positions that she could observe.

Ada, however, was unable to follow his suggestions. Complications after a bout with measles in

1829 left her legs paralyzed. For a year she could neither stand nor walk. But, during her long convalescence, she did continue lessons. Having the opportunity to study uninterrupted was the one good thing Ada could find in being an invalid.

Her great sorrow, though, was her inability to go horseback riding. "I want very much to see the Dun Mare again, and still more to be upon her nice comfortable back," she wrote her mother, who was staying in London.

Ada made extremely slow progress toward recovery. She was kept absolutely immobile, and her muscles became weak as a result. After a year, she was able to sit up for only half an hour a day. A year after that, she still required crutches. It was three years before she could walk without feeling dizzy.

During this time, she developed a phobia about sleeping in a bed. Instead, she would wrap herself in a blanket and curl up on the floor or on the sofa. Perhaps it was the long period of being an invalid or perhaps the time she spent in childhood lying immobile on a board that made her prefer the floor.

Long after her recovery, Ada continued to correspond with Frend. She had a soft spot in her heart for him in spite of the fact that he scoffed at new concepts in mathematics. She once wrote asking about rainbows. "I am very interested on the subject just now, but I cannot make out one thing at all, viz: why a rainbow always appears to the spectator to be an arc of a circle. Why is it a curve at all, and why a circle rather than any other curve?"

Ada's studies were not limited to science. She also developed her talent at drawing and became an acceptable artist. She sang, she mastered the piano, the violin, and the harp, and she even learned to play the guitar. She did not, however, like opera. Her reaction to the leading lady in *Anna Bolena* annoyed her mother. Ada considered it absolutely absurd for a woman to fall down in a faint, then get up and start singing again.

Horseback riding, that other accomplishment of the well-bred young lady, was her first love. From the time she first climbed onto a horse, she was an enthusiastic rider. At the age of twenty, she confessed that being on a leaping horse was the greatest pleasure she knew, "even better than waltzing."

Growing up, Ada had been surrounded by her mother's friends and had had little association with persons her own age. In spite of Ada's isolation, Lady Byron complained that her teenage daughter argued too much and that her greatest ambition was to be popular.

Ada's messy habits also grated on Lady Byron's nerves. Finally, unable to stand her daughter's untidiness, she turned to her physician, William King, for help. Lady Byron admired Dr. King for his religious views. He shared her belief that God had put evil in the world so that people could learn to be good. She was quite correct in assuming that the doctor would pass these views on to Ada. He did so in long, dreary, sermonlike letters.

In her instructions to Dr. King, Lady Byron set out a clear objective. Ada's "greatest defect [is] want of order—for this the Mathematical science would perhaps form the best remedy." It pleased her greatly two weeks later to report that Dr. King had "commenced . . . operation on Ada's brain."

Five years later, eighteen-year-old Ada echoed her mother's words when she wrote to Dr. King asking his advice. "I find that nothing but very close & intense application to subjects of a scientific nature now seems at all to keep my imagination from running wild. . . . If you will do me so great a favour as to give me the benefit of your advice and suggestions as to the plan of study most advisable for me to follow, I shall be most grateful."

Dr. King replied with one of his moralizing lectures. He told her she was correct in assuming that her chief resource and safeguard was a course of severe intellectual study. "For this purpose there is no subject to be compared to Mathematics and Natural Philosophy."

Such a study, he said, would require complete attention and follow a natural pattern the mind could comprehend. Best of all, mathematics had no connection with feelings. He recommended not only a set of books but a method of study that would keep her mind from straying even during her daily walks.

Ada loved intensive study, and soon asked Dr. King some geometry questions which had puzzled her. Her questions unnerved him. Dr. King considered mathematics good for disciplining the mind but little else. He sent her another lecture outlining the necessity of conventional study. "You will soon puzzle me in your studies. When I was at College . . . we got up a set of books and seldom went out of them. . . . Loose reading does no good, especially in early life. . . . You must trammel your mind in these things. . . . Some day I shall point out to you a system of Logic, & Morals, but it would be now premature."

Premature or not, Ada's original thinking was beyond the doctor's comprehension. On the subject of geometry, she remarked, "I do not consider that I know a proposition until I can imagine to myself a figure in the air, and go through the construction & demonstration without any book or assistance whatever."

The effort to cure Ada's untidiness turned out

to be a dismal failure. Yet it was precisely her ability to imagine things in her mind that helped her understand relationships others never considered.

Chapter / Five

The Thinking Machine

By the end of adolescence, Ada had become a beauty. She was slender and of medium height. An acquaintance described her as having "a fine form of countenance, large expressive eyes, and dark curling hair. Her features bear a likeness to her father's, but require some observation before it appears strongly."

When John Hobhouse, Byron's friend, met Ada for the first time, his reaction was not so kind. He recorded in his diary, "She is a large coarse-skinned young woman, but with something of my friend's features, particularly the mouth. I was exceedingly disappointed."

At seventeen, Ada was at the age when young women were presented to society. "Coming out" meant attending a series of parties that included an introduction to the king and queen. It also signaled

Ada in her coming-out dress

a young woman's readiness for marriage.

Lady Byron did not live a fashionable life, but she knew that her daughter had to take part in the "season" in London in order to meet eligible men.

By this time Ada had thrown away her crutches. Although her mother worried that she was still too frail, Ada was eager to attend the fancy balls. Lady Byron fussed over her daughter's dresses. "I find myself obliged to give more thought to this matter than I had wished in order to prevent her from being called upon to do so," she wrote.

When Ada, dressed in white stain and tulle, finally entered the drawing room at St. James Palace for her presentation to King William IV and Queen Adelaide, on May 10, 1833, her mother was exceedingly pleased.

It was natural for Ada to be nervous when presented to the king and queen, but once that feeling wore off, she had a wonderful time at the ball that followed. Those who watched her dance found little trace of the illness that had kept her crippled for so long.

After being cooped up for years surrounded mostly by her mother's sober friends, Ada was enchanted. She enjoyed the music and was thrilled at the opportunity to meet some of the great personalities of the day. She appreciated the duke of Wellington's straightforward manner of speaking and found the duke of Orleans charming.

Three weeks later, at another social event, Ada finally met the man who would challenge her mind.

Charles Babbage, mathematician and inventor, was almost the same age as Ada's mother. His wife had died several years earlier, and hostesses eagerly sought him as a guest because he was a wonderful storyteller and had a sharp wit.

As a child, he had been curious about everything and took apart each new toy to find out what was inside.

At school, he discovered a room full of books. The joy they brought him made Babbage an advocate of having libraries in every school. He devoured the books on mathematics and learned so much math that when he got to college he knew more than his tutors.

At Cambridge, he met John Herschel, son of the famous astronomer William Herschel, the discoverer of the planet Uranus. John Herschel was an astronomer in his own right, and he later became known for cataloging stars in the southern hemisphere. Babbage and Herschel became lifelong friends, and together founded the Analytical Society, which brought advances in mathematics to the university.

Shortly after leaving Cambridge, Babbage married Georgiana Whitmore and became a teacher of mathematics. In 1816, just three months after Ada was born, he became a fellow of the Royal Society of London, the most prestigious organization of English scientists. Four years later he helped found the Royal Astronomical Society.

Babbage had an insatiable interest in puzzles and gadgets. He constructed mechanical toys for his children, including a "telephone" system for sending written messages in little cylinders running along a wire. He also created an infallible device for picking locks, and a system for deciphering codes.

Soon after the Royal Astronomical Society was established, Babbage was working with Herschel checking mathematical calculations that had already been made for the society. It was a tedious task. As they worked, they found many discrepancies between their numbers and the ones listed previously. Exasperated, Babbage blurted out, "I wish to God these calculations had been executed by steam."

Herschel looked up from the table of numbers in front of him, thought a moment about the prospect of a machine doing the calculations, and calmly replied, "It is quite possible."

Herschel's challenge started Babbage on his quest. Later the inventor gave two other accounts of the moment when the idea for the machine

Inventor Charles Babbage

came to him, but they all related to the same thing—to find some way to end the errors and mind-numbing work of producing tables of numbers. The Difference Engine, a machine that would calculate numbers without making any errors, began to take shape in Babbage's mind and in his workshop.

In 1822, while Ada was still collecting tickets for good lessons, Babbage displayed a model of his first calculating machine. It had a series of toothed disks with the numbers 0 to 9 printed on the rims. The independently turning disks were stacked on columns. To add two numbers together, the operator set each number on a column, then connected the columns with gears. As the crank was turned, the teeth meshed, and the columns turned until all the zeros were lined up. The number produced on a third column was the answer.

Babbage called his machine the Difference Engine because numbers were calculated by adding the difference between two successive entries in the table to the next successive number.

The Royal Astronomical Society gave the inventor a gold medal and praised him for being able "to perform singly the work of a multitude, with the accuracy of a select few by mechanism which takes the place of manual labour."

In 1823, at the urging of the Royal Navy, the

government began funding development of a full-size Difference Engine. Britain was then the world's greatest sea power, and the navy needed accurate navigational tables to guide its ships.

Work on the machine went slowly. Special tools had to be made before it could be constructed. Serious arguments developed between Babbage and his engineer, and as a result the engineer dismissed the workers, who left with all the tools. (At that time, tools belonged to the workmen, even if they were paid for by the builder.)

Babbage had estimated that it would take three years to complete the Difference Engine. Instead, fourteen years passed, and, with the machine 90 percent complete, Babbage finally proposed that the Difference Engine be abandoned. He decided that it would be easier and less expensive to start all over and build a new machine he called the Analytical Engine. Rather than being just a calculator like the Difference Engine, this one would "analyze" its action as it proceeded through the calculations. It would stop in a sequence of operations, store information, calculate data needed for the next step, retrieve the previous information, and continue to the end of the problem.

The government balked, having already spent £17,000 on the Difference Engine. Some law-

Babbage's Difference Engine

makers favored the new machine, but others ridiculed the idea.

While waiting for the government to make up its mind, Babbage remained a charming guest and a brilliant host. On Saturday evenings as many as 200 guests crowded into his London house at 1 Dorset Street. His hearty laugh and enthralling tales captivated the company.

Early in the summer of 1833, two weeks after meeting Babbage, Ada and her mother were among the guests at his house. One of the curiosities attracting everyone's attention was the model of the Difference Engine. Babbage obligingly gave demonstrations. He enjoyed mystifying his guests with the "thinking" machine, whose answers seemed to come like magic.

Few of the visitors took the time to examine the mechanism, but Ada studied the gears, rods, and toothed wheels until she understood how the machine worked.

The middle-aged inventor and the young debutante were still several years away from close friendship, but the seed had been sown. Babbage's Analytical Engine, successor to the Difference Engine, would draw their lives together.

Chapter / Six

Thrush, Hen, and Crow

After the excitement of her first London season, Ada was eager for more freedom. In an effort to get her mother to consider her as an adult, she wrote a "declaration of independence":

"After a child grows up, I conceive the parent who has brought up that child to the best of their ability, to have a claim to his or her gratitude. . . . But I cannot consider that the parent has any right to direct the child or to expect obedience in such things as concern the child only."

This spirit of independence led Ada to try to elope with a young man who had been hired as her tutor. When she arrived at his house, however, his mother notified Lady Byron, and Ada was promptly returned home.

Renewed lectures on being godly and subservient to her mother poured forth. These came from all directions—her mother, her mother's three best friends, whom Ada called the Furies, and her governess. The only person Ada ever talked to about the attempted elopement, though, was Woronzow Greig, the son of her new tutor.

This tutor was a safe one, and well qualified. Mary Fairfax Somerville was a respected scientist. In her youth in Scotland, she had been discouraged from trying to learn, and she deeply resented women's lack of educational opportunities. She "thought it unjust to give women a desire for knowledge if it were wrong to acquire it."

While reading a ladies' magazine one day, the young Mary had discovered some strange symbols. Her brother's tutor explained that the article was about algebra. She quickly persuaded the tutor to buy her some mathematics books. She studied in private because everyone, particularly her father, discouraged her from learning subjects they considered useless, even harmful, for girls.

When Mary Fairfax married Russian naval captain Samuel Greig, she found even less sympathy, but she refused to give up her studies. After Captain Greig died, she married William Somerville, a medical doctor who enthusiastically encouraged his wife. Before long, she had translated an important and complicated astronomy book. Later she wrote her own book, called

The Connection of the Physical Sciences.

The Royal Society, that staid group of gentlemen scientists, broke tradition and elected Mary a member. The society honored its first woman member by placing a bust of her in its meeting hall. But Mary Somerville never got to walk past her statue. Women were not allowed to attend meetings at the Royal Society.

Mrs. Somerville saw no need to complain. Always pleasant, she went right ahead being a mathematician, a housewife, and a mother to her son and two daughters.

Eighteen-year-old Ada read her new tutor's work, and the woman scientist became her ideal. Mary's son, Woronzow Greig, became Ada's close friend.

Mrs. Somerville was determined that her daughters would not be denied the opportunity to study as she had been. She took them to science lectures as well as to the opera. Ada went along on some of their excursions and sometimes spent the night at her tutor's house. The inquiring attitude she found in the Somerville house contrasted with the heavily moralistic atmosphere of her own home.

Up to this time, women had not been allowed to attend scientific debates. But when King's College opened in 1832 as part of the University of

Mary Somerville. In an era when learning was considered bad for women, Ada's tutor earned the respect of England's most eminent scientists.

London, there were remarkably few restrictions on those attending. Women asked to be allowed to hear some lectures on geology, and their request was supported by many scientists, including Charles Babbage. Permission was granted, but when women flocked to the lectures, the bishop of London called a halt to their attendance on the grounds that females were too delicate for weighty scientific matters.

Before the ban went into effect, however, Mrs. Somerville and her daughters, as well as Ada and her governess, heard a scientist explain Babbage's Difference Engine.

After studying over a year with Mary Somerville, Ada was pleased with her progress as a mathematician. Still, she faced the prospect of being labeled an old maid if she did not marry soon. Then, through Woronzow Greig, she met William King. Greig felt his college friend would make an excellent husband for Ada. William was not related to Lady Byron's doctor, who had the same name. He was a bachelor with very reserved manners. At thirty, he was eleven years older than Ada.

Although he was a member of the aristocracy and owned two estates, William King did not have a large income. One estate, Ockham Park, he had inherited as the eighth Baron King. The other was a smaller place called Ashley Combe in southwest

England. Neither estate provided a large income for William because they had to support several members of his family.

Greig arranged to bring his friend to his mother's house during one of Ada's visits. William King fell in love with the dark-haired beauty, and they became engaged almost immediately. Three days after Ada had accepted his proposal, William nervously wrote, "Since we parted I have been in [a] state of continued intoxication of delight at the prospect held out to me by our interviews on Thursday."

He worried about making Ashley Combe acceptable for her, even though it was beautifully situated on the Somerset coast. His letter continued: "I am endeavouring to make this hermitage (for it is little more) less impossible in its appearance, & to make it in short not unworthy some time of your presence. The scenery is the only thing that can so entitle it, for within doors it is of the most humble description and it is in the state which most homes are which have not been inhabited for fifteen years."

The formal, courteous King was just the sort of man Lady Byron could admire. He was educated and had traveled on the continent. While working with his uncle in the British government office in Greece, he had posed for a portrait dressed as a

Greek national. Lady Byron did not seem to resent the fact that both the costume and the pose bore a striking resemblance to the portrait of her own husband that had been banished from the mantel at Kirkby Mallory Hall.

During the month-long engagement, Lady Byron employed seamstresses to prepare a splendid trousseau for the nineteen-year-old bride. Ada's dowry was generous, but the terms of it left Ada with only £300 a year to spend as she chose. Everything else, including lifetime use of the Wentworth estate, which Ada would inherit from her mother, would belong to her husband.

Ada resented the pittance she was allowed. Her pin money was exactly the same amount that Lady Byron had received when she married. Ada felt this was unjust, but William did not seem to think so. He expected to take care of everything for her.

On July 8, 1835, Ada and William were married in the drawing room of Fordhook, Lady Byron's London residence. *The World of Fashion* reported the whole affair in its marriage column. "The fair Augusta Ada Byron, 'Ada, sole daughter of my house and heart,' has become the wife of Lord King."

Lady Byron could not have been more pleased with her new son-in-law. She immediately made herself part of the new family, frequently taking charge of things. Far from resenting his mother-in-law's interference, William became her devoted follower. He had an abiding dislike of his own mother, who he said had been cruel to him as a child, and he was not on speaking terms with her or with his brothers.

Lady Byron took William under her wing and filled a great gap in his life. William made a point to consult her about his many architectural and agricultural projects. Ada, whose whole life had been run by her mother, made no objections.

Pet names began to appear in the frequent letters that went back and forth between Lady Byron and the newlyweds. "Dear little Canary bird," wrote her mother to Ada the day after the wedding, "may the new 'cage' be gladdened by your notes." Ada had been called bird names such as "Thrush" since childhood. Now Lady Byron became "Hen," and because of his dark eyes, William was designated "Crow."

During Christmas of their first year together, the newlyweds received a package from Lady Byron. To Ada's surprise, it was the long-hidden portrait of her father. She, of course, had never seen the picture because of the stipulation in her grandmother's will. Now that Ada was married, she was considered an adult, making it proper for her to

The long-hidden portrait of Lord Byron dressed as an Albanian nobleman

have the portrait.

For the first time, she learned what her father looked like. By this time, she had read his poetry, but his name had never been mentioned in her presence. Seeing the picture, Ada began to realize how much her father meant to her.

Chapter / Seven

In Search of Something More

Less than a year into her marriage, Ada was expecting her first child. When the healthy boy was born on May 12, 1836, he was named Byron at Lady Byron's request. The new grandmother was ecstatic and took charge in her usual way. Unbelievably, the nurse she hired for her grandchild was Grimes, the very nurse who had been dismissed after taking such gentle care of Ada during her chicken pox.

After her first child was born, Ada was able to enjoy the pleasure of horseback riding only briefly before pregnancy forced her to stop again. A year and a half after young Byron was born, a girl arrived. The bright, happy child, born on September 22, 1837, was named Anne Isabella for her grandmother, and like her namesake, came to be called Annabella.

Shortly after her daughter's birth, Ada became desperately ill with cholera. Against odds, she survived, but she never fully recovered her health.

Lady Byron was ambitious for her son-in-law and wanted him to become a member of Parliament. During Coronation Honors for Queen Victoria on June 30, 1838, William King took his seat in the House of Lords with the title first earl of Lovelace. He had chosen the name from one of Ada's seventeenth-century ancestors, Lord Lovelace of Hurley, whose peerage had died out. Ada became countess of Lovelace.

A year later, Ada's last child was born, on July 2, 1839. The boy was named Ralph in memory of Ada's beloved grandfather.

Although some of Ada's letters to her mother reveal that she loved her children, she resented their claims on her time. "I am not naturally or originally fond of children," she wrote, "& tho' I wished for heirs, certainly should never have desired a child."

Lovelace's own unhappy childhood made it difficult for him, too, to relate to his children. In his letters he complained of their impertinence and persistent disregard of rules. In contrast, in his letters to his wife, he often sounds like a loving father speaking to a child.

Lovelace shared with Ada a love of animals.

He and his wife were excellent equestrians and spent much time riding at their estates. Lovelace was proud of his stable of fine animals and made sure they received only the finest care. One of his rare complaints about Lady Byron was that she drove his carriage horses too long and hard.

Although a horseman, Lovelace was not a hunter and claimed that farming was a healthier and more beneficial activity than riding to hounds. He prided himself on his farms and took an active interest in his tenants.

His consuming interest, however, was architecture. He bought an estate near Ockham Park called East Horsley and began a series of projects that consumed both his time and his money. The estate was renamed Horsley Towers when he turned the house into a medieval-like castle. One of the improvements at Horsley involved the beams that supported the roof of the great hall. An avid reader of architectural journals, Lovelace had discovered a new method of shaping timber. He built the necessary airtight steam box to soften the wood, and produced unusual curved beams that were admired by the leading architects of the day.

At Ashley Combe, on the Bristol Channel, Lovelace built a harbor. Ada loved sailing, and he bought a boat for her. He also constructed an area for swimming in the ocean water.

For the most part, Lovelace conceived these projects as ways to amuse himself. While they cost a great deal of money, most of it supplied by Ada's dowry, family comfort and well-being was not the driving force behind them. Annabella complained that her father refused to install a bathroom at Ockham Park because it cost too much to pump the water. This refusal came despite the fact that doctors had prescribed hot baths as a cure for some of Ada's ailments.

Lord Lovelace greatly admired his mother-in-law for her work among the poor, and he imitated some of her projects. He was so impressed with the Ealing Grove school she had established that he started a similar one at Ockham Park.

Attempts at teaching his own children, however, met with little success. The tutors Lady Byron provided seemed to come and go with great regularity. For a while, both Ada and her husband tried working with the children themselves. Yet Ada had little patience for teaching and Lovelace even less. He was particularly upset over the way his older son slouched.

Even before her children were of school age, Ada explained to a prospective tutor that she believed she was not meant to teach but to direct operations. "You will not wonder that I begin to feel them occasionally (to speak plainly but truly) a real nuisance. . . . I believe I am fit to educate, with proper aids. But . . . as the chief, the general." Her children at the time were ages four, three, and one.

Ada's interest in education really centered on her own. She wanted to return to her study of mathematics. Surprisingly enough, both her mother and husband went out of their way to give her time to do that. Lovelace indulged her by taking care of their country estates, leaving Ada to reside in London, where she could pursue her studies. Lady Byron kept the children—usually one at a time. She was appalled at the manners shown by her grandchildren and spent much time trying to improve them.

Some time earlier, Ada had turned to Charles Babbage to help her find an instructor. "[I have] made up my mind to have some instruction next year in Town, but the difficulty is to find the *Man*. I have a peculiar way of learning & I think it must be a peculiar man to teach me successfully."

The celebrated inventor replied with a compliment but sidestepped the hint for his services. "I think your taste for Mathematics is so decided that it ought not to be checked. I have been making enquiry but cannot find at present anyone at all to recommend to assist you. I will however not forget the search."

In 1840 Ada began studying mathematics with

Augustus De Morgan, a professor of mathematics at the University of London. De Morgan's brilliant wit and love of puzzles and riddles motivated his students. Besides writing numerous encyclopedia articles, he produced several excellent books on arithmetic, algebra, trigonometry, and calculus. Much of his fame resulted from the relationship he saw between logic and mathematics.

Ada's letters to De Morgan were filled with far-ranging questions. He was very impressed by her ability, but he believed that her intense pursuit of mathematics would lead to a breakdown. He felt, as did many in that day, that a woman's delicate nervous system could not stand the strain of concentrated study.

While Ada corresponded with De Morgan, Babbage waited for the government to make up its mind about funding his machine. Two years after Ada's initial letter asking for a mathematics tutor, she began to cultivate a real friendship with Babbage. Lovelace was delighted because he too enjoyed the inventor's genial manner and interesting discussions of politics and economics. Babbage was one of the few persons with whom he was completely at ease.

Early in January 1841, Ada invited Babbage to visit them at Ockham Park. She begged him to stay more than just three nights because "I must show

Augustus De Morgan. The famous mathematician was impressed with Ada's intellect but feared for her "delicate" female nervous system.

you a certain book called my Mathematical Scrap-Book."

She quickly followed this letter with another advising him to bring a warm coat to wear in the open carriage and not to forget his ice skates. At the end, she got to the main purpose of the visit— she was anxious to put her mind at his service in regard to his machine. "Some day or other you will have to put me in possession of the main points relating to your engine."

Both Ada and her husband had great faith in Babbage and his calculating machine. They hoped to use their influence to get the necessary funding for its construction, and Babbage welcomed their interest.

Ada was eager to make a contribution to science, but her pursuit was interrupted that spring when Lady Byron summoned her to Paris for a shocking revelation. Medora Leigh, a person Ada thought was her cousin, was introduced as her half sister. The truth of Medora's paternity is uncertain, but Lady Byron chose to believe the story of Byron's incest with his half sister. In a great show of forgiveness, Lady Byron declared Medora part of her family.

While Ada was in Paris, her mother provided dresses for Ada's presentation at the French court. With great satisfaction Ada reported to her husband, "The Hen is giving the Bird Plumage!" Court appearances required ball dresses, which ordinarily had to be bought with Ada's limited pin money. After returning home, she remarked, "Court

Dresses & Trains, & all the vanities of life. I think they will be nearly settled in a day or two. I am arranging all my dresses & coiffures for the season, & then I shall have some always ready, & no more plague about it."

Ada was determined to resume her studies. Her husband and mother were indulgent, as usual. Writing to her son-in-law, Lady Byron wryly remarked, "Love to the bird when you can insinuate it between two problems."

The opportunity for Ada to demonstrate her excellent education, her intense interest in mathematics, and her wide-ranging imagination was about to present itself.

Chapter / Eight

The Mathematical "Child"

The year prior to Ada's trip to Paris, Babbage had spent a number of months on the Continent. The major purpose of his 1840 trip was to attend a meeting of Italian scientists.

At Turin, on the Po River within sight of the Alps, mathematicians and engineers gathered to discuss the latest scientific ideas. For several years Babbage had refused requests to lecture on his calculating engine because he felt it was not ready. This time, he showed up with drawings, plans, and notebooks.

At the sessions Babbage talked about his Analytical Engine. Among those listening and observing was a young Italian military engineer named Luigi Federico Menabrea, a man who later became the prime minister of Italy.

Babbage explained the superior features of his

new machine. Unlike the Difference Engine, which worked straight through a problem, the Analytical Engine could make some calculations, store them, analyze what to do next, and then return to complete the problem.

Babbage wanted an official report on the Analytical Engine to be written by an eminent scientist. Such an endorsement would give the machine credibility and perhaps help Babbage get past his stalemate with the British government. Instead, the engineer Menabrea became the author.

In his paper, Menabrea explained how the machine worked. His task was made difficult by the lack of an actual machine. He had to work solely from Babbage's drawings, which used Babbage's own system of engineering drawing notation. Menabrea found it necessary to consult with the inventor often about details.

At last, Menabrea finished the description of how the machine operated and produced some tables as explanatory material. Two years after the conference, Menabrea's article, written in French, appeared in the October 1842 issue of *Bibliothèque Universelle de Genève.*

Shortly afterward, Charles Wheatstone, a lecturer and scientist known for his experiments in electricity, approached Ada about a translation of

In later years, a portion of Babbage's Analytical Engine was constructed by the inventor's son, Henry. He followed his father's original drawings.

the Menabrea article for the British journal *Taylor's Scientific Memoirs*. As a family friend of the Lovelaces, he knew Ada's facility with both French and mathematics.

By the fall of 1842, Babbage was aware that Menabrea's article had been published, but he did not know that Ada had been asked to translate it. When he found out, he suggested that she write a completely new article. Ada declined but was receptive to the idea of adding notes to fill out what Menabrea had written.

Ada's health during the time she worked on the notes continued to deteriorate. She suffered from digestive problems and had bouts of asthma. Her doctors had prescribed some medicines that we recognize as dangerous substances today. Opium, often in the form of laudanum, was a common narcotic available to ladies with "nervous" temperaments. Ada took it with wine.

She suffered radical mood swings, ranging from severe depression to sudden frantic bursts of energy and elation. Often her mind would race uncontrollably. At times she could not even hold a pen to write. She complained of seeing visions. Her face and body would swell enormously, and her eyes burned. She shivered during the cold winters.

The effect of the medicines may account for some of her claims of fantastic abilities. Ada wrote her mother, "I believe myself to possess a most singular combination of qualities exactly fitted to make me pre-eminently a discoverer of the hidden realities of nature. . . . Firstly: Owing to some peculiarity in my nervous system, I have perceptions of some things, which no one else has; Secondly: my immense reasoning faculties; Thirdly: my concentration faculty . . ."

Ada believed she was fulfilling her destiny by explaining Babbage's machine. Her reasoning may have been cloudy because of the influence of drugs, but her concentration was not hindered. Characteristically, she threw herself into the translation as intemperately as she did everything else. And the notes she added to the translation contained perceptions of "hidden realities" that went beyond a simple explanation of how the machine operated.

As Ada worked on the translation of Menabrea's article, she realized that Menabrea had explained only the mathematical principles that made the machine work, what she called its "legislative" features. She also wanted everyone, particularly the British government, to understand its mechanical operations and practical applications, what she called its "executive" features.

As usual, Babbage continued to improve his machine even as Ada worked. Ada made changes in the Menabrea text to reflect the current state of the machine and used footnotes to alert the reader that changes had been made.

Ada felt the need to explain the machine more fully than Menabrea had, but as a translator she could not add anything to his text. Babbage's suggestion that she add notes suited her perfectly. She not only expanded Menabrea's twenty pages but also posed ideas of her own, ideas that sometimes spoke of radical new uses for the machine beyond its original purpose of generating accurate tables of numbers.

The notes, numbered A through G, were placed at the end of the translation. They were not organized in any particular way and made no attempt to give a complete explanation of the machine. Perhaps that was why, when Ada was nearly finished, Babbage suggested that she write an organized description featuring not only the machine's mathematical features but also the functions it could perform. Ada was too anxious to see her first work in print to follow the suggestion.

She never doubted, however, that she was capable of such a description if only her health would hold up. Early in July 1843, she wrote Babbage, "That brain of mine is something more than merely Mortal; as time will show; (if only my breathing & some other etceteras do not make too rapid a progress *towards* instead of *from* mortality). Before ten years are over, the Devil's in it if I haven't sucked out some of the life-blood from the mysteries of this universe."

In spite of exaggerated claims for her mind and half jokes about her health, Ada continued to labor over the plans and drawings of the Analytical Engine. Extensive correspondence went back and forth between Ada and Babbage, clearing up sticky points.

In several of the notes Ada compared the machine to a Jacquard loom. In the early 1800s

The Jacquard loom, controlled by a chain of perforated cards, provided a model for Charles Babbage's calculating machine. As Ada wrote: "We may say most aptly, that the Analytical Engine weaves algebraic patterns just as the Jacquard-loom weaves flowers and leaves."

Joseph Marie Jacquard had perfected the use of punched cards to weave patterns on cloth. The cards, arranged in a certain sequence, produced the pattern by dictating which crosswise threads (the *woof*) would run over and under lengthwise threads (the *warp*) of a piece of cloth. Using a separate card for each weaving instruction, it produced very intricate patterns.

The Jacquard loom was a technological breakthrough and had earned its inventor a pension from Napoleon. As early as 1836, Babbage had written to Mary Somerville that he was using punched cards with his calculating machine, an idea that came from his knowledge of the Jacquard loom.

As Ada worked intently on her notes, she began to refer to them as her "first child." This "child" took her from periods of highest exultation to complete despair.

At Babbage's suggestion she expanded or created new tables to complement the ones presented by Menabrea. She worked the tedious calculations for the tables only to find that she had made some mistakes and had to do them again. In the process of checking the material, she even caught Babbage in some errors.

She worked doggedly, occasionally going horseback riding to clear her mind. "I am working very hard for you, like the Devil in fact; (which perhaps I am). I think you will be pleased."

Babbage sent many compliments. "It is your usually clear style and requires only one trifling

French inventor Joseph Marie Jacquard

alteration which I will make," he wrote on one occasion, referring to one of her notes. Either she had missed some point or he had made another change without telling her.

Illness plagued Ada that summer, and her temper became short when Babbage dared to change something she had written. "And you have made a pretty mess & confusion in one or two places, . . . where you have ventured . . . to insert or alter a phrase or word; & have utterly muddled the sense." She softened this by saying, "I fear you will think this is a very cross letter. Never mind. I am a good little thing, after all."

Somewhere along the way, Ada dropped the formal salutation of "My dear Mr. Babbage." Instead, letters began "Dear Babbage." This unheard-of familiarity was almost equivalent to calling the inventor by his first name.

During this period of feverish activity, Ada's children were watched over by their father and grandmother. Lovelace was proud of his wife's work and had joined the Royal Society, which by now had opened its doors to gentlemen other than scientists. From him Ada gained access to the society's information, but, of course, she couldn't go to meetings herself.

Wheatstone had set a deadline to submit the translation in order to get it printed. As time grew short, Ada juggled her time, making last-minute additions to her writing, sending pages for Babbage's comments, and correcting proofs from the printer.

Just as Ada was finishing her work, she and Babbage had a serious disagreement. He asked her to include a section that would present his side of the quarrel with the British government. He wanted the prestige of *Taylor's Scientific Memoirs* to boost his claim.

Ada angrily refused and called Babbage selfish for wanting to interject something else in her work. The disagreement was settled when the editor agreed to publish the "Statement of the Circumstances Attending the Invention and Construction of Mr. Babbage's Machines" in another of Taylor's journals.

In the final hectic days of writing, Ada fussed over her pages and even dared to tell respected scientific publisher Richard Taylor that he was to be diligent that "every particular care & accuracy be observed."

When delivered to the printers, Ada's notes were nearly three times as long as Menabrea's original article. Babbage could only comment, "The more I read your notes, the more surprised I am at them."

Chapter / Nine

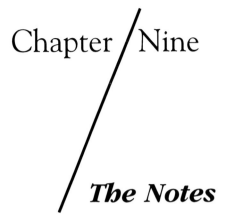

The Notes

Ada's notes are a combination of mathematics and propaganda. The Lovelaces, along with other prominent individuals, wanted the government to fund Babbage's project. Ada intended her notes not only to explain the machine but also to win support for it.

Note A

Ada recalled the value of the Difference Engine as a calculator, then moved on to the superior features of the new Analytical Engine. As she set forth this machine's ability and usefulness, she made it clear that the Analytical Engine was not merely an improvement on the first machine. The Difference Engine could produce error-free calculations but was limited to problems of addition, while the Analytical Engine could do all four arithmetical operations. Also, the new machine, unlike the

Difference Engine, could stop in the middle of an operation, determine the next step, and proceed until the solution was reached.

Punched cards controlled the action of the machine and allowed it to break down a complex problem into a series of smaller operations.

There were different kinds of punched cards. Operation cards told the machine to add, subtract, multiply, or divide. Another kind, called variable or instruction cards, governed the machine's actions and told it where to store calculations. Once the programmer set the cards to perform a particular activity, the machine internally analyzed data and determined what steps were necessary to complete the task.

Actual calculation took place in a part of the machine called the *mill*. Results were stored on the Variable columns in the *storehouse* to be used in later calculations, or they became the final answer.

The punched cards were similar to those used by the Jacquard loom. "We may say most aptly, that the Analytical Engine *weaves algebraical patterns* just as the Jacquard-loom weaves flowers and leaves," stated Ada.

In thinking about the machine's possibilities, Ada took one of her intuitive leaps. She understood the machine's ability to recognize mathematical symbols. Her musical background led her to

speculate that with proper mathematical operations it could play music. "Supposing, for instance,
that the fundamental relations of pitched sounds in
the science of harmony and of musical composition
were susceptible of such expression and adapta-
tions, the engine might compose elaborate and scientific pieces of music of any degree of complexity
or extent."

Before leaving Note A, she returned to her
main purpose—to urge the British government to
end its indecision. What a shame it would be, she
chided, if the present generation were "acquainted
with these inventions through the medium of pen,
ink, and paper [only]." What a blow to England's
reputation and honor if there should be a "completion of the undertaking by some *other* nation or
government."

Note A covered thirteen pages. One gargantu-
an sentence of 158 words praised mathematics
because it "constitutes the language through which
alone we can adequately express the great facts of
the natural world."

Babbage read Note A and praised the
"admirable and philosophic view" of the Analytical
Engine. "Pray do not alter it," he said.

Note B
Menabrea had written that the Analytical

Engine would be immense. Ada described it as having an indefinite number of columns, at least 200 as compared to 7 for the Difference Engine. These columns, with as many as 30 or 40 independently turning disks on each one, constituted the machine's *storehouse*.

Ada drew a diagram to represent the rows of columns and included squares and circles to record what was happening on a column. In the circle at the top, a plus or minus indicated whether the number was positive or negative. The square at the bottom contained "a memorandum for the observer, to remind him of what is going on." The squares Ada described are equivalent to the comments or remarks [REMs] programmers use today to explain what action is taking place. They were not part of the operation itself.

Note B again described the work of the punched cards. Then, at the end of the note, Ada hailed the machine for making clear the various steps needed to analyze and solve a problem in mathematics, "how clearly it separates those things which are in reality distinct and independent, and unites those which are mutually dependent."

Note C

In Note C, Ada recommended a trip to see the Jacquard loom in operation. At both the Adelaide

Gallery and the London Polytechnic Institution, weavers worked constantly on the loom and were available to answer questions.

Ada explained an important simplification that allowed the Analytical Engine to use fewer cards than the Jacquard loom, which had a separate punched card for each instruction. Cards in the Analytical Engine could return to their original position in a process called *backing*. A card or set of cards could be used as many times as needed "bringing any particular card or set of cards into use *any* number of times successively in the solution of one problem."

In today's computer programming, the *backing* process is called a *do-loop*.

Note D

Note D clarified the mechanics of the machine by giving a fuller explanation of two tables in the Menabrea text. These tables showed the functions of three kinds of Variable columns, always identified with a capital V in order to distinguish them from a mathematical variable. One kind of Variable column contained data. Another kind held temporary information that would be used later. A third kind received the final results.

Ada added a third table to help describe how the columns worked. Her table plus both of

Menabrea's tables "form a complete and accurate method of registering every step and sequence in all calculations performed by the engine."

Ada also noted that more than one sequence could lead to a calculation's solution. The goal was to find the procedure that used the least amount of time. She reminded the reader that several sets of operations often went on at the same time, independently doing related work.

As she finished Note D, Ada was near exhaustion from her fever-pitch activity. Babbage sent his usual compliment.

Note E

Note E drove Ada to distraction. It gave a complicated example of how the machine worked through a problem. She explained how cards returned to their original position in a recurring set of actions she called *cycles*. There could even be cycles within cycles.

In the ten-page note, Ada described characteristics still seen in modern computers. In the Babbage machine, stacks of punched cards, working in the manner of modern function keys, controlled the machine. Repetitions (do-loops she called *backing*) allowed the same cards to be used for repeated operations. Conditional responses equivalent to "if-then" statements in today's terminology instructed the machine on successive steps.

Ada reminded the reader that it is easy to think of the machine merely as arithmetical because it produced its results in numerical notation, but it was also algebraic. It could give answers in symbols as well as numbers if the printing mechanism were set up to do so.

Note F

In Note F, Ada emphasized the simplicity of the Analytical Engine as compared with the Jacquard loom and provided an example of how 3 cards could take the place of 330 cards, or even "thousands or millions of cards."

Ada also thought the machine could solve problems that had not been worked out before, especially ones that were almost impossible to compute. She cited astronomical tables as an example.

In addition, she said the Analytical Engine might even provide some mathematical amusement by generating random numbers, such as are used today in sequencing action in computer games. She didn't dwell on this possibility very long for fear that the idea of generating numbers rather than solving mathematical problems might sound frivolous.

Note G

In Note G Ada warned, "The Analytical Engine has no pretensions whatever to originate anything. It can do whatever we know how to order it to perform. It can *follow* analysis; but it has no power of *anticipating* any analytical relations or truths." She was aware that it was simply a machine that needed human action to set it in motion.

It occurred to her that individuals, through the analysis required to set information on the machine, might come up with new discoveries. Insight into old problems and solutions for new concepts would come from manipulating information in a less traditional manner.

She then summed up the machine's characteristics:

1. It could add, subtract, multiply, or divide any numbers.
2. There was no limit, theoretically, to the magnitude or quantity in the numbers it could act upon.
3. It combined numbers and quantities both arithmetically and algebraically.
4. It used algebraic signs according to their proper laws.
5. It could substitute any formula for another one.

6. It could provide for numbers such as those that pass through zero or infinity.

The bulk of this long note details how the machine could be programmed to compute a complex sequence of numbers. Ada chose as her example the calculation of the Bernoulli numbers, which have no easily recognizable sequence pattern. Some are positive numbers, some are negative, and every other one is zero.

In a letter to Babbage she stated, "I want to put in something about Bernoulli's numbers, in one of my Notes, as an example of how the implicit function may be worked out by the engine, without having been worked out by human head & hands first. Give me the necessary data & formulae."

The final page of Ada's work was the diagram that was the program she wrote showing how to compute the Bernoulli numbers. Babbage much later claimed to have done the diagram himself, but Ada's letters reveal that she put it together. She took the information and formulas he supplied and in her capacity as programmer determined where to set the calculations on the machine and where to display results.

Work on the diagram caused Ada great mental effort, and her health continued to deteriorate. Finally, though, she was able to send Babbage the

good news. "Lord L— is at this moment kindly ink-
ing it all over for me. I had to do it in pencil."

Interestingly enough, because she had no
machine on which to try the program, there are a
couple of programming errors in the printed edi-
tions available today. *Debug*, of course, was not in
Ada's vocabulary. One of the errors could possibly
have been a printer's mistake, and she had complained to Babbage about it. Two others, however,
seem to have been programmer errors. In 1889,
when Henry Provost Babbage, the inventor's son,
published a book about his father's work, it contained those errors.

Ada's notes are impressive. Besides expanding
on Menabrea's article, they show her extraordinary
flights of imagination. Ada proposed uses for the
Analytical Engine that not even the inventor had
considered. Twenty years later, long after Ada's
death, Babbage made an assessment of Menabrea's
article and the notes added by Ada. "These two
memoirs taken together furnish . . . a complete
demonstration."

Chapter / Ten

Unfulfilled Ambitions

Ada's efforts were published in *Taylor's Scientific Memoirs* in August 1843. The credit line stated that Menabrea's "Sketch of the Analytical Engine Invented by Charles Babbage, Esq." was translated, with notes, by "A.A.L."

As a proper Victorian lady, Ada didn't want to sign her name and had, at her husband's suggestion, used her initials to remain identifiable.

Menabrea was baffled when Babbage's son showed him the translation. The Italian engineer could not recall any mathematician with the initials "A.A.L." He was most surprised to learn the author was the wife of an English earl.

Ada purchased 250 copies of the translation and sent them to friends and prominent scientists. Most of them had known she was working on the project.

Mary Somerville reviewed her copy and praised Ada's proficiency with mathematics and the "clearness with which . . . [she had] illustrated a very difficult subject." Privately, she worried about Ada's health.

Augustus De Morgan was similarly impressed by Ada's work. In a complimentary letter to Lady Byron, he expressed the feeling that Ada would have matched or surpassed students at his alma mater, Cambridge. "I feel bound to tell you that the power of thinking . . . Lady L. has always shown from the beginning of my correspondence with her, has been something . . . utterly out of the common way for any beginner, man or woman."

He even ventured to say that Ada eclipsed Mary Somerville in the originality of her thinking. He felt that Ada's ability to grasp mathematical principles would have made her "an original mathematical investigator, perhaps of first-rate eminence, if she had been able to study at the university." At the same time, he conceded that such inventiveness would have kept her out of the highest ranks of students, since Cambridge did not encourage creativity.

The letter in which he expressed these opinions also carried grave concerns about Ada's health. He believed, as many did, that women could not stand the strain of prolonged mental activity. Steady and strenuous thinking and study-ing, he thought, required a man's constitution. Whatever De Morgan's assessment, it was some-thing more deadly than mental activity that even-tually claimed Ada's life.

As her work on the Notes concluded, Ada looked for the next project on which to focus her energies. After explaining the Analytical Engine, she wanted to see it built.

The same month that the translation appeared in print, Ada approached Babbage in one of her omnipotent moods. "I must now come to a practi-cal question respecting the future. *Your* affairs have been & are deeply occupying both myself & Lord Lovelace. . . . I have plans for you." Those plans required Babbage to concentrate his efforts solely on completing the Analytical Engine while Ada or someone else agreeable to him would have com-plete control of his business matters.

Continuing the sixteen-page letter, Ada launched into a sermon on God, Truth, and Glory, calling herself one of the divine prophets. At the end she asked Babbage to come to Ashley Combe to discuss what they would do next. "I wonder if you will choose to retain the lady-fairy in your ser-vice or not."

Babbage came for a visit, but never pursued her plans. His wide-ranging, inventive mind could not be hobbled any more than her imagination could be. He remained a welcome guest at Ashley Combe and Horsley Towers, but he and Ada never cooperated on anything else.

The deathblow to Babbage's hopes for the Analytical Engine came two months after Ada's translation was published. The government sent him notice regretting that they had to abandon the machine on which so much ingenuity and work had been spent. As a result, the Analytical Engine was never built, and Babbage spent the rest of his life working with other models of his calculating machine.

Ada's health continued to be a concern. She suffered a variety of problems, some of which were never diagnosed. Sometimes she felt terrible thirst. At other times she described episodes when her "whole throat & face suddenly swelled to an enormous size, & I felt as if threatened with instant annihilation." These incidents left her face disfigured. Even her doctor spoke about her "mad" look.

Ada was treated with various medicines. Finding that opium was not working, the doctor tried morphine. "I think he has got the thing at last," Ada reported to her mother. "I must tell you that latterly—the last 2 or 3 years—Opium had seemed strangely to disagree with me. But I now understand why this has been. . . . I was all the time taking wine or other stimulant; & the 2 things made a terrible jumble."

She wrote a friend that she wanted to use her terrible experience with the combination of opium and wine to let the world know how such a combination affected the brain. "I have my hopes, & very distinct ones too, of one day getting cerebral phenomena such that I can put them into mathematical equations; in short a law or laws for the mutual action of the molecules of the brain."

As usual, Ada's ideas outstripped the scientific techniques of her day, and in this case even those of the twentieth century. Within the last fifty years, mathematical models have been developed to show the workings of some parts of the body—for example, the muscles. The brain, however, is too complex to be reduced to available mathematical models.

Lady Byron passed off Ada's illnesses as treatable and felt her daughter was better off keeping her mind busy in some field of science. When De Morgan had mentioned his worry about Ada, her mother replied that if Ada "would but attend to her stomach, her brain would be capable even of more than she has ever imposed on it. . . . The consciousness of making progress in science seems to me an essential element in her happiness, & appears [no less] desirable to Lord Lovelace than to myself."

Lovelace was eager for his wife to continue her work. He was immensely proud of her. In spite of continuing rumors of her strange behavior, he tried to make her appear to society as normal as possible. A letter he wrote a year after Ada's translation was published described a small dinner gathering at their house. Ada performed on the harp, and her husband noted that his guests "must be struck with the grandeur & nobleness of her intellect—she has but to be natural to be as much loved as she is to be admired and wondered at." Gossip surrounded his wife, who often lived apart from him, and this brief interlude gave him a chance to present her as a charming hostess.

As time went on, though, the rumors increased. Lord Byron's old friend John Hobhouse recorded in his diary that a dinner companion leaned over and "in a whisper, asked me if she [Ada] was not mad." This annoyed Hobhouse, who considered his friend's daughter an interesting conversationalist. Ada's preference for seclusion, however, coupled with her habit of saying things just to startle her listeners, only fueled the reports.

Aged twenty-seven when she completed her translation, Ada was determined to continue to use her genius. She reported to her mother that she was "the Deborah, the Elijah of Science. . . . a Prophetess born into the world." She was convinced that her "first born," as she referred to the Notes, would "make an excellent head I hope of a large family of brothers and sisters."

Unsure where to concentrate her efforts, Ada explored several scientific areas. She wrote Babbage that she was considering a paper about Georg Simon Ohm's work with electricity. Wheatstone suggested she do more translations, but she was not proficient in German, the language in which most scientific papers were written, at that time.

About a year after the publication of the Menabrea translation, Ada went to visit Andrew Crosse, a middle-aged scientist whose house was near Ashley Combe. Crosse was experimenting with electromagnetism, and Ada was interested in conducting an experiment with the muscles of frogs.

This time it was Ada who complained about the chaos of a household. She described the house as "the most *unorganized* domestic system I ever saw." She was particularly put out by the location of the water closet (bathroom). The room was situated so that anyone going there had to walk in front of everyone else, and sometimes the door was locked and Ada had to call for the key!

Crosse himself had "the most utter lack of system even in his Science," but soon Ada felt she

could remain at his house "a fortnight with advan-
tage. . . . Old Crosse delights in my quizzing
him. . . . Young Crosse is an excellent mathematician . . . & he works my brain famously for he
opposes everything I advance, intentionally; but
with perfect good humor. . . . He will be an addition
to my catalogue of useful & intellectual friends."

At the Crosse house, Ada found no science
project to work on, but a suave, self-serving man
joined her "catalogue" of friends. In a web so tan-
gled that its complexity became known only on her
deathbed, Ada Lovelace's life became entwined
with that of Andrew Crosse's son, John.

Chapter / Eleven

Compulsive Gambling

In 1845, Ada was almost thirty years old and having difficulty finding direction for her life. To Woronzow Greig, her friend and confidant, she made shocking revelations about her marriage.

Just a few months after telling her mother that Lovelace was a good husband, that "all the *angles* are rubbing down more and more," she confided to Greig that marriage for her was a *"life-less life."* She was quick to add, "It is not his fault that to me he is nothing whatsoever, but one who has given me a certain social position. Unfortunately, every year adds to my utter want of pleasure in my children. . . . Poor things! I am sorry for them."

The children had been under their grandmother's guidance since Ada started work on Menabrea's translation. As time when on, Byron, now called Viscount Ockham, became so difficult to control that his father put him in the navy at the age of thirteen to teach him discipline. Annabella spent time on the Continent with her governess, and Lady Byron took complete control of Ralph.

Ada attempted some other scientific projects but without success. Wheatstone's proposal that she apply for the position of science adviser to Prince Albert, Queen Victoria's consort, came to nothing. She improved her German enough to produce a draft review of a pamphlet on magnetism, but it was never published. Her final effort was to add a set of mathematical footnotes to one of Lovelace's essays published in the *Journal of the Royal Agricultural Society*.

Ada made no effort to avoid the growing gossip linking her to other men. Dr. James Phillips Kay, an admirer, was struck by her beauty and eccentricity. He admitted to Lady Byron that he named Ada "Will-o'-the-wisp" because of her "waywardness, beauty & intangibility."

Lovelace, an aristocratic, considerate, but stodgy husband, was remarkably unperturbed by his wife's activities. He served as lord lieutenant of Surrey, enjoyed the construction projects at his estates, and continued his participation in the House of Lords. More than that, he wrote his wife and mother-in-law almost every day they were apart.

Greig warned Ada about the damaging rumors that were being spread by newspaper reports. One newspaper gossiped: "The resemblance of Lady Lovelace to her renowned father, beyond some parental likeness, has as yet been confined to a certain amount of eccentricity. Her ladyship from her whimsical notions is thought a little daft. Lady Lovelace thinks so highly of the opinion of Mr. Frederick Knight . . . that she does not fancy even her costume complete until it has received the sanction of his acknowledged taste."

Ada shrugged it off. She had enjoyed her rides with Frederick Knight, and she responded, "I went on riding with him rather more particularly after I heard the report in question."

Ada's acquaintance with John Crosse had begun innocently enough when he escorted her from Ashley Combe to his father's house a little over a year after Ada's translation was published. "Our horses absolutely flew. . . . I never saw the poor things go so beautifully." She filled the rest of her letter with a description of the horses. In the end, horses were the very thing that led her, with Crosse's help, into nightmarish debt.

There is no record of when Ada started gambling at the racetrack. Some have speculated that the mathematical book she was anxious to show Babbage was a betting system she and Crosse had worked out. Since the book is lost, there is no proof, but it probably was a scrapbook of problems, solutions, and puzzles such as most mathematicians of the day kept.

It is true that Ada's bets were placed through her personal maid, Mary Wilson. A lady of Ada's standing could not be seen in the company of gamblers. And Mary, who had worked for Babbage, came to the Lovelaces with his recommendation.

Babbage knew Ada was gambling, but he was not her companion in this activity. That was John Crosse. The Lovelaces accepted him as a social equal, only later finding out that the man they thought was a bachelor concealed a family elsewhere and lied to cover the fact. Ada and Crosse became part of a ring of gamblers.

By 1848 Ada was so deeply in debt that she turned to her friend Greig. He helped arrange a bank loan of £500 without her husband's knowledge. Ada thanked the banker, explaining that her need was caused by "the *very small* sum (considering my inheritance and position), which was settled on me upon marriage."

When the banker suggested she ask Lovelace for an increase in her pin money, she explained that he had incurred heavy expenses from his building projects. Eight months later, even more in debt, she told Greig that Lovelace had declined to raise her allotment to £500 but that he had paid one bill and was going to pay for her court dresses. The explanation she gave to Lovelace for her money shortage was that she had overspent on books and music. Some of the money had actually been used to buy furniture for Crosse's house.

Ada was terrified that Lady Byron would learn of her money problems. "If she knew of the debt it would do irreparable mischief in more ways than one."

By 1849 her debts had nearly doubled, and she had no way to pay them. She could not conceal her betting from Lovelace any longer. He gave her £100 and offered to take to court the person threatening her, even though he knew extortion cases were hard to prove.

In August 1850, believing that all the debts were cleared, Lovelace took his wife on a long holiday. As they toured around the English countryside, he wrote to Lady Byron almost daily, giving descriptions of grand homes and churches and news of the various people they visited.

He chose his words very carefully when they reached Newstead Abbey, Lord Byron's ancestral home, which Ada had expressed a desire to see. Sticking to the safe subject of architecture, the faithful son-in-law described the excellent restoration done by the current owner. Byron's room had been left untouched.

On first seeing Newstead, Ada fell into a great depression, causing her host some concern. Speaking to him about her emotions, however, made her feel a strange sense of kinship to the place. A visit to the Byron vault nearby sealed her resolve to be buried next to her father.

Never one for caution, she informed her mother, "I do love the venerable old place & all my wicked forefathers!" Her enthusiasm brought a sharp protest from Lady Byron, who considered it a reflection against her own character. Ada, of course, protested that she had been misinterpreted.

After a few more days of sight-seeing, Lovelace ventured off to see more cathedrals before joining Ada at the Doncaster races. Later Lady Byron would use this action to charge Lovelace with abandoning his wife to the clutches of gamblers, but by now Ada was beyond saving.

The situation looked innocent enough. Their hosts owned a famous racehorse named Voltigeur, who won a thrilling race. Lovelace reported to his mother-in-law that Ada "has distinguished herself much by naming some of the winners merely from seeing them paraded before the stand & judging from points before the race began."

Ada may have convinced Lovelace that she picked by appearance alone, but she probably had

Newstead Abbey, Lord Byron's ancient seat

tips. Whatever her system, it wasn't foolproof, and she lost on Voltigeur.

Lovelace, who fell victim to pickpockets, found the place distasteful. The worst thing about racetracks, he grumbled, was the people they attract.

Ada, however, continued to gamble after she returned home. Through her maid Mary she received tips and placed disastrous bets. She loved long odds and seemed to think she had a system that could not fail. She knew the work of Jakob Bernoulli, who is given credit for being one of the developers of the Theory of Probability, but her choices frightened even some of the bookies. One refused to take any more bets from her, and another warned that she had little chance of winning.

Nothing deterred her. Derby Day, May 21, 1851, added a staggering £3,200 to Ada's debts. As she met with her gambling partners to settle, she was able to satisfy her debtors because Lovelace had given her a letter saying that he would cover her debts. He was completely unaware just how compulsive his wife's gambling had become.

Another disaster struck that spring. The condition of Ada's health became so alarming that her husband called in a doctor. The diagnosis was cervical cancer.

Chapter / Twelve

The Mournful Cavalcade

Lovelace went immediately to see his mother-in-law to let her know about Ada's condition. Added to his despair was the unpleasant task of telling her about Ada's gambling. Lady Byron, relying on her own doctor's diagnosis, assumed Ada's health was no worse than usual. But the gambling she could not forgive, and she held Lovelace responsible. She demanded to see Ada for an explanation, but Lovelace begged off, saying that Ada was in too delicate a condition for her mother to visit. Lady Byron turned on him in a cold fury.

Ada was not informed about the cancer and remained optimistic about her recovery. She missed being able to ride, though, and prescriptions for painkillers gave her little relief. The debts continued to hang heavy. Lovelace consoled her, "Do not be disquieted dearest about pecuniary matters for I hope and trust that some day we may be relieved from our present difficulties."

In private agony over Ada's deteriorating health and huge debts, Lovelace now faced the rejection of the mother-in-law he had admired. In addition, Lady Byron owned the lease on Lovelace and Ada's London house and had loaned them money to pay for the furniture.

Lovelace tried to keep up normal appearances. He encouraged guests whose company Ada enjoyed. Babbage was especially welcome, with his interesting conversation and creative projects. Lovelace noted that his wife still "mastered the mathematical side of a question in all its minuteness."

Unfortunately, other, less desirable men made their way to 6 Great Cumberland Place. John Crosse came frequently, and Ada turned to desperate measures to cover the losses that continued to mount as she secretly placed bets. The members of her betting ring worked out a complicated arrangement in which they took out life insurance to cover their debts to one another. John Crosse held the letter Lovelace had given Ada to cover her debts at the 1851 derby.

Lady Byron continued to blame Lovelace for Ada's gambling. In March 1852 she sent a lawyer to interview her daughter. Shocked to see Ada so ill, he gently probed for information about her debts. He reported to her mother, "I *believe* I have obtained a correct List." Lady Byron sent money for their payment, but Ada had secrets that neither her husband nor her mother knew.

Still unable to face her mother, Ada wrote, "I have a great desire to see you; & yet a great dread. I fear your not being fully aware of the extremely delicate condition I am in, & how one *breath* that was painful to me might have a severe effect on my much shaken health."

Lady Byron came anyway, and eventually Ada confessed that she had pawned the Lovelace diamonds for £800, about a third of their value. It had cost another £100 to have paste diamonds made to replace them so Lovelace would not suspect anything. Lady Byron promptly redeemed the diamonds and restored them without Lovelace's learning of their absence. The paste diamonds went into her lockbox.

Ada's pain became so intense that she could not sleep more than an hour or two, but she was determined that an artist complete her portrait. With a steel will, she sat at the piano, holding her hands on the keys so the painter could get them right. Lovelace, in the journal he was keeping about his wife, noted how she and their daughter Annabella enjoyed some moments playing duets.

On August 3, 1852, after another portrait sitting, Lovelace revealed to Ada that Crosse had a wife and family. Ada must have known already, but now that Lovelace knew as well, it would be awkward for her betting accomplice to visit.

That evening Crosse came to the house. Ada, in physical agony and terrified of disclosure, gave Crosse the heirloom diamonds a second time. The eight £100 notes he received from the pawnbroker the next day may have covered some betting debts, but, more important to Ada, they also bought his silence. Lovelace knew about the betting, but he never suspected that Crosse's frequent visits with Ada were anything other than friendship.

In the midst of this turmoil, Ockham returned home from the navy. Ada suddenly revived at the sight of her oldest child. A week later, though, the doctor informed her that her condition was hopeless. When his mother told him she was dying, Ockham begged not to be sent back to his ship. Forced to go, he stuffed his midshipman's clothing in a duffel bag, sent it to his father, and disappeared.

When Ada learned of her condition, she called her husband into her room and told him that she wished to be buried beside her father. Perhaps as a premonition, Ada also set forth her wishes about who was to get her personal things. Babbage was to

Ada's last portrait

have any twelve titles from among her books, and she asked him specifically to see that her servants received some money. "Dear Babbage," she wrote, "In the event of my sudden decease before the completion of a will I write this letter to entreat that you will *as my executor* attend to the following directions; 1stly you will apply to my mother for the sum of £600. . . . 2ndly you will go to my bankers . . . and obtain from them my account & balance. . . . 3rdly you will dispose of all papers & property deposited by me with you. . . . In the fullest reliance on your faithful performance of the above, I am Most sincerely & affectionately yours Augusta Ada Lovelace."

Babbage had no chance to act on Ada's instructions. Lady Byron, who had been visiting Ada almost daily, moved in on August 20 and refused entrance to all but her own friends. The household servants were dismissed, and Babbage was turned away at the door.

Lovelace, trying desperately to mend relations with Lady Byron, let her take charge, but he did what he could to comfort his wife. Ada requested a visit from Charles Dickens, whose books she enjoyed, and Lovelace welcomed the famous author. He brought Fanny Kemble's sister to sing for her. When Ada could no longer descend the stairs for dinner, her bed was set up downstairs, and he placed pots of geraniums in the doorway so she could see them.

Lady Byron kept an icy distance from Lovelace. She accused him not only of letting her daughter engage in disastrous gambling but also of turning Ada against her. He tried to show his mother-in-law the diary that spoke of his care for Ada and his regard for Lady Byron. She had by now twice redeemed his family heirloom in transactions he knew nothing about, but it was the rift with her daughter she could not forgive.

Ada's death seemed imminent. Lovelace recorded that she "was so angelic, the character of her beauty so pure and disengaged from bodily elements that she was quite fit to pass away from among us into a higher sphere of existence."

It would have been much better for her and for Lovelace if that had happened, but Ada grimly hung on. She would, she said, live long enough for Ralph to make it home from Hofwyl in Switzerland, where he by then attended school. Annabella bathed her mother's face and hands. Lovelace sat beside her bed and recalled their rides over the countryside. Lady Byron took her turn at the bedside when Lovelace was away and sketched Ada in one of her rare moments of peace.

Just as Lady Byron had insisted that sedatives be withheld so that the pain could cleanse her daughter's soul, she now insisted that Ada confess her sins. On the first day of September, Lovelace was shattered by Ada's faltering admission of an affair with John Crosse.

In a house heavy with unhappiness, Lovelace and his mother-in-law waited. After three more months of unspeakable agony, Ada died on November 27, 1852. Lovelace wrote, "All is at last over after incessant suffering until quite the end when her spirit passed away so quietly that those about her did not perceive for some moments after, that she was gone. This was at 9.30 last Evg."

The *Times* of London carried the notice of Ada's funeral on December 3:

> The remains of the Countess of Lovelace, the daughter of the late Lord Byron, arrived at Nottingham on Thursday by the Midland Railway from London. It having become known that the deceased lady was to be interred in the Village Church of Hucknall Torkard, in the vault where lie the remains of the Noble Poet, a vast number of persons were assembled to witness the funeral. . . . The mournful cavalcade was met at the Church Gates by the Rev. Curtis Jackson, who read the burial service. . . . The coffin of the deceased Countess is covered with violet-coloured velvet, the handles being solid silver. Upon the lid is the escutcheon of the Earl of Lovelace (in silver) and at the head and foot are massive silver coronets.

Lady Byron did not attend her daughter's funeral. Lovelace kept his promise: Ada's coffin touches that of her father.

And there she lay for a hundred years, unknown.

Epilogue

The immediate aftermath of Ada's death was nearly as painful as her lingering illness. Babbage tried to carry out Ada's requests, only to be instructed by Lady Byron to return all of Ada's papers and letters. He sent a stiff refusal. "With respect to the collections of letters and papers given by Lady L. to Mr B. during her life as well as an extensive correspondence carried on with her for years, many parts of which are highly creditable to her intellect, Mr B. feels entirely at liberty to deal with them in any manner he may choose. The conduct of Lady L's relatives to Mr B. has released him from the feeling of delicacy towards them; and Lady L's testamentary letters give him full authority." He never got the books she left him.

John Crosse, however, already had the locket containing Byron's hair, his gold ring, and a miniature portrait of the "Maid of Athens." Ada had smuggled these things out to him just as her mother arrived to shut the door on his visits. After Ada's death, he claimed the insurance policy Ada had taken out to cover her debts with the gambling ring. Because he held over a hundred intimate letters from her, he was paid off by Ada's family. The letters he returned were burned.

Lovelace remained estranged from his children. About ten years after Ada's death, he married again, and his second wife sought to heal the rift between the children and their father.

Ockham, the oldest, despising the pretensions of the upper class, changed his name to John Okey and spent the rest of his life working as a laborer. He died of tuberculosis at the age of twenty-six, never reconciled to his family.

Annabella, called Anne as an adult, was reared chiefly by her grandmother, and remembered her father as a stern man. She was a brilliant student who became fluent in several languages, especially Arabic. She married a well-to-do landowner named William Blunt, and her spirit of adventure led her to obscure places. She inherited her parents' love of horses and developed a stable of famous thoroughbreds. When she died, her sister-in-law said of her, "To the end of her life she had the heart of a child, the brain of a scholar and the soul of a saint."

Ralph lived with Lady Byron from the age of nine and took the name Milbanke at her request. He loved the mountains and developed a passion for scaling sheer rock faces and traversing glaciers. As an adult, he spent the summer months conquering snow-covered peaks in the Swiss Alps. When his older brother died, he became heir to all the family's titles. He refused to speak to his father even though both were members of the House of Lords. On his father's death, he became the second earl of Lovelace.

Lady Byron survived her daughter by eight
years and never reconciled with her son-in-law.
Ralph inherited her estates, but her papers did not
come to him for many years. When they did, he
spent nearly the rest of his life putting them in
order, a difficult task because so many were undat-
ed.

The world forgot about Ada Byron Lovelace
until 1954, when a researcher found her work.
Even though more recent students of her life have
found a mathematical error in her translation of
Menabrea's article, the mistake does not diminish
her most important accomplishment: She envi-
sioned multiple uses for a machine she never saw.

In 1974 the United States Department of
Defense decided to certify one computer language
for all of its tasks. Six years later, on Ada's 165th
birthday, the Ada Joint Program Office was created
to introduce and support the Ada computer language. Shortly afterward, the American National
Standards Institute approved Ada as a national all-
purpose standard and gave it document number
MIL-STD-1815, honoring the year of Ada
Lovelace's birth.

Charles Babbage would have approved.

Appendix
Ada Byron Lovelace: A Time Line

December 10, 1815	Augusta Ada Byron born
January 1816	Lady Byron takes Ada and leaves husband
April 25, 1816	Byron leaves England
1822	Lady Noel, Ada's grandmother, dies
April 19, 1824	Byron dies in Greece
1826–1828	Ada tours Continent with mother
May 1829	Measles attack leaves Ada unable to walk
May 10, 1833	Ada's presentation at court
June 5, 1833	Ada meets Babbage
June 1833	Lady Byron and Ada at Babbage's house
Spring 1834	Mary Fairfax Somerville becomes Ada's tutor; Ada meets Somerville's son, Woronzow Greig
July 8, 1835	Ada marries William King
May 12, 1836	Byron Noel (later Viscount Ockham) born
September 22, 1837	Anne Isabella (called Annabella, later Lady Anne Blunt) born
June 30, 1838	William King created Lord Lovelace
July 2, 1839	Ralph Gordon Noel King (later Ralph Milbanke) born
June 1840	Ada begins to study with Augustus De Morgan

August 1840	Babbage goes to Turin to present lecture on Analytical Engine
October 1842	Menabrea's article published in *Bibliothèque Universelle de Genève*
August 1843	Ada's translation and notes published in *Taylor's Scientific Memoirs*
November 1844	Ada meets John Crosse
May 1, 1848	Ada secures loan to cover gambling debts
Summer 1848	Ada adds equations to Lovelace's article "On Climate in Connection with Husbandry"
1849	Lovelace pays some of Ada's gambling debts
August 1850	Ada and husband on long tour
September 1850	At Newstead Abbey; Ada goes to Doncaster races
May 21, 1851	Ada loses £3,200 on Derby Day
Summer 1851	Ada has severe hemorrhages; doctor diagnoses cancer; Lady Byron asked not to visit
March 1852	Lady Byron pays Ada's gambling debts
Summer 1852	Lady Byron redeems pawned Lovelace diamonds
1852	Lovelace keeps journal of wife's illness
August 12, 1852	Ada asks Babbage to be executor of her will

August 20, 1852	Lady Byron comes to take charge of house; dismisses servants
November 27, 1852	Ada dies
December 3, 1852	Account of Ada's burial beside her father
1860	Lady Byron dies
1862	Ockham (John Okey) dies
1864	Lovelace remarries
1871	Babbage dies
1893	Lovelace dies
1906	Ralph, earl of Lovelace dies
1917	Lady Anne Blunt dies

/Sources

Unable to search manuscript collections myself, I have used secondary sources that have direct quotes in them. All secondary sources are listed, but four contained the bulk of the quotes. Unfortunately for my purposes, each had defects, especially ellipses that may have contained useful information for this biography. As a note, I too have used ellipses, which may or may not have been in the source I used.

Primary sources:

Lovelace Papers, Bodleian Library, Oxford University

Somerville Papers, Bodleian Library, Oxford University

Babbage Papers, British Library, Additional Manuscripts, London

Major secondary sources:

Baum, Joan. *The Calculating Passion of Ada Lovelace.* Hamden, Conn.: Archon Books, 1986. Only source of comments on Ada's notes appended to translation of Menabrea's article. Problem with imprecise or missing source of quotes.

Elwin, Malcolm. *Lord Byron's Family: Annabella, Ada, and Augusta, 1816–1824.* Edited from the author's typescript by Peter Thomson. London: John Murray, 1975. Close, careful account, third of a series based on the Lovelace Papers, finished by Thomson after Elwin's death. Deals largely with Lady Byron and Augusta Leigh, with Thomson's additions giving most of the information about Ada.

Moore, Doris Langley. *Ada, Countess of Lovelace: Byron's Legitimate Daughter.* London: John Murray, 1977. Author, with two published Byron biographies, displays great aversion to Lady Byron.

Stein, Dorothy. *Ada: A Life and a Legacy.* Cambridge, Mass.: MIT Press, 1985. Author discovered an error in Ada's translation and from that extrapolated Ada's lack of mathematical ability.

Additional sources:

Babbage, Charles. *Passages in the Life of a Philosopher.* London: 1864.

Babbage, Henry Provost. *Babbage's Calculating Engines.* 1889. Reprint. Los Angeles: Tomash, 1982.

Buxton, Harry Wilmot. *Memoir of the Life and Labours of the Late Charles Babbage Esq. F.R.S.* Edited and with introduction by Anthony Hyman. Cambridge, Mass.: MIT Press, 1988.

Dubbey, J. M. *The Mathematical Work of Charles Babbage.* Cambridge, England: Cambridge University Press, 1978.

Hyman, Anthony. *Charles Babbage, Pioneer of the Computer.* Princeton, N.J.: Princeton University Press, 1982.

Lovelace, Mary, Countess of. *Ralph, Earl of Lovelace: A Memoir.* London: Christophers, [1920].

Mayne, Ethel Colbun. *The Life and Letters of Anne Isabella, Lady Noel Byron.* London: Constable, [1929].

Menabrea, L. F. "Sketch of the Analytical Engine Invented by Charles Babbage," from the *Bibliothèque Universelle de Genève*, October 1842, no. 82. With notes upon the Memoir by the Translator Ada Augusta, Countess of Lovelace, [1844]. Reprint. In *Charles Babbage and His*

Calculating Engines. Edited by Philip and Emily Morrison. New York: Dover, 1961.

Newman, James R., ed. "Commentary on Augustus De Morgan." In *The World of Mathematics*, vol. 4, 2366–2368. New York: Simon & Schuster, 1956.

Strickland, Margot. *The Byron Women.* New York: St. Martin's Press, 1974. No documentation for quotes.

Chapter 1: Child of Fame and Discord
8: "Sunday last"—Moore, p. 5.
12: "Princess of Parallelograms"—Mayne, p. 53.
13: "How wonderful"—Moore, p. 24.
13: "a little encumbered"—Moore, p. 24.
13: "the child was born"—Mayne, p. 198.

Chapter 2: "Ada, Sole Daughter of My House and Heart"
16: "Only a few days ago"—Elwin, p. 167.
17: "I give her"—Elwin, p. 145.
17: "It would be imprudent"—Moore, p. 8.
18: "I am sadly"—Elwin, p. 144.
20: "That young Lady"—Elwin, p. 148.
20: "Her passions"—Moore, pp. 17–18.
21: "Kettle's crying"—Moore, p. 18.
21: "My daughter is"—Stein, p. 22.
21: "My eldest little girl"—Stein, p. 22.

Chapter 3: No Weeds in Her Mind
22: "There are no weeds"—Strickland, p. 194.
22: "The great thing is to be"—Elwin, p. 168.
23: "I want to please"—Stein, p. 24.
25: "Perhaps by the time"—Moore, p. 20.
26: "disposition, habits, studies"—Moore, p. 21.

26:   "Ada's prevailing character"—Moore, p. 22.

Chapter 4: Proper Education
31:   "education by action"—Mayne, p. 489.
31:   "The sons of the wealthy"—Mayne, p. 489.
32:   "'imagination,' 'wonder'"—Moore, p. 62.
35:   "I want very much"—Moore, p. 29.
35:   "I am very interested"—Moore, p. 54.
36:   "even better than waltzing"—Moore, p. 231.
37:   "greatest defect"—Baum, p. 15.
37:   "commenced operation"—Baum, p. 15.
37:   "I find that nothing"—Stein, pp. 42–43.
37:   "For this purpose"—Stein, p. 43.
38:   "You will soon puzzle"—Stein, p. 45.
38:   "I do not consider"—Baum, p. 29.

Chapter 5: The Thinking Machine
41:   "a fine form"—Moore, p. 32.
41:   "She is a large"—Moore, p. 53.
42:   "I find myself obliged"—Moore, p. 40.
44:   "I wish to God"—Buxton, p. 46.
46:   "to perform singly"—Buxton, p. 77.

Chapter 6: Thrush, Hen, and Crow
50:   "After a child"—Stein, p. 33.
51:   "thought it unjust"—Stein, p. 47.
55:   "Since we parted"—Moore, pp. 65–66.
56:   "The fair Augusta Ada"—Moore, p. 71.
57:   "dear little Canary"—Moore, p. 72.

Chapter 7: In Search of Something More
60:   "I am not naturally"—Stein, p. 64.
62:   "You will not wonder"—Stein, p. 66.
63:   "[I have] made up my mind"—Moore, p. 95.
63:   "I think your taste"—Moore, p. 96.
64:   "I must show you"—Moore, p. 96.
66:   "Some day"—Moore, p. 96.

66: "The Hen is giving"—Moore, p. 125.
66: "Court Dresses"—Moore, p. 162.
67: "Love to the bird"—Moore, p. 131.

Chapter 8: The Mathematical "Child"
71: "I believe myself"—Stein, p. 86.
73: "That brain of mine"—Moore, p. 158.
75: "I am working"—Stein, p. 106.
75: "It is your usually"—Baum, p. 77.
77: "And you have made"—Stein, pp. 108–109.
78: "every particular care"—Baum, p. 85.
78: "The more I read"—Baum, p. 86.

Chapter 9: The Notes
The unidentified quotations in this chapter are taken from Ada's translation of Menabrea. The source examined is a reprint and paging is slightly different from the original.

81: "admirable and philosophic"—Stein, p. 101.
87: "I want to put in"—Stein, p. 106.
88: "Lord L— is"—Stein, p. 108.
88: "These two memoirs"—Babbage, Charles, p. 136.

Chapter 10: Unfulfilled Ambitions
90: "clearness with which"—Baum, p. 85.
90: "I feel bound"—Stein, p. 82.
91: "I must now"—Moore, pp. 163–165.
92: "whole throat & face"—Moore, p. 215.
92: "I think he has got"—Moore, p. 214.
93: "I have my hopes"—Moore, pp. 215–216.
93: "would but attend"—Stein, pp. 81–82.
94: "must be struck"—Stein, p. 164.
94: "in a whisper"—Stein, p. 181.
94: "the Deborah"—Moore, p. 219.
95: "make an excellent"—Baum, p. 89.
95: "the most *unorganized*"—Stein, p. 145.
95: "the most utter lack"—Stein, p. 146.

Chapter 11: Compulsive Gambling

Chapter 12: The Mournful Cavalcade

Epilogue

Selected Bibliography

Babbage, Charles. *Passages in the Life of a Philosopher.* London: 1864.

Babbage, Henry Provost. *Babbage's Calculating Engines.* 1889. Reprint. Los Angeles: Tomash, 1982.

Baum, Joan. *The Calculating Passion of Ada Lovelace.* Hamden, Conn.: Archon Books, 1986.

Buxton, Harry Wilmot. *Memoir of the Life and Labours of the Late Charles Babbage Esq. F.R.S.* Edited and with introduction by Anthony Hyman. Cambridge, Mass.: MIT Press, 1988.

Elwin, Malcolm. *Lord Byron's Family: Annabella, Ada, and Augusta, 1816–1824.* Edited from the author's typescript by Peter Thomson. London: John Murray, 1975.

Lovelace, Mary, Countess of. *Ralph, Earl of Lovelace: A Memoir.* London: Christophers, [1920].

Mayne, Ethel Colbun. *The Life and Letters of Anne Isabella, Lady Noel Byron.* London: Constable, [1929].

Menabrea, L. F. "Sketch of the Analytical Engine Invented by Charles Babbage," from the *Bibliothèque Universelle de Genève,* October 1842, no. 82. With notes upon the Memoir by the Translator Ada Augusta, Countess of Lovelace, [1844]. Reprint. In *Charles Babbage and His Calculating Engines.* Edited by Philip and Emily Morrison. New York: Dover, 1961.

Moore, Doris Langley. *Ada, Countess of Lovelace; Byron's Legitimate Daughter.* London: John Murray, 1977.

Newman, James R., ed. "Commentary on Augustus De Morgan." In *The World of Mathematics,* vol. 4, 2366–2368. New York: Simon & Schuster, 1956.

Stein, Dorothy. *Ada: A Life and a Legacy.* Cambridge, Mass.: MIT Press, 1985.

Strickland, Margot. *The Byron Women.* New York: St. Martin's Press, 1974.

/Index